The Psychology of Industry

First published in 1921 and revised here in 1947, *The Psychology of Industry* was intended to make available for the ordinary person, rather than specialists in either psychology or economics, the results of recent experimental work in psychology at the time, so far as these had a direct bearing on problems of industry and commerce. The revised edition intended to emphasize principles, rather than details, to bring out the relation of psychology to economics, and of education to industry. Stress is also laid on the new urgency which the Second World War had given to many of the problems discussed. Today it can be read in its historical context.

This book is a re-issue originally published in 1921. The language used is a reflection of its era and no offence is meant by the Publishers to any reader by this re-publication.

I0095477

The Psychology of Industry

James Drever

Routledge
Taylor & Francis Group
LONDON AND NEW YORK

First published in 1921
by Methuen & Co. Ltd
Second edition, revised, 1947

This edition first published in 2025 by Routledge
4 Park Square, Milton Park, Abingdon, Oxon, OX14 4RN

and by Routledge
605 Third Avenue, New York, NY 10017

Routledge is an imprint of the Taylor & Francis Group, an informa business

© 1921 James Drever

Publisher's Note
The publisher has gone to great lengths to ensure the quality of this reprint but points out that some imperfections in the original copies may be apparent.

Disclaimer
The publisher has made every effort to trace copyright holders and welcomes correspondence from those they have been unable to contact.

A Library of Congress record exists under LCCN: 47007780

ISBN: 978-1-032-91713-9 (hbk)
ISBN: 978-1-003-56458-4 (ebk)
ISBN: 978-1-032-93151-7 (pbk)

Book DOI 10.4324/9781003564584

THE PSYCHOLOGY
OF INDUSTRY

by

JAMES DREVER
M.A., B.Sc., D.Phil.
EMERITUS PROFESSOR OF PSYCHOLOGY IN THE
UNIVERSITY OF EDINBURGH

SECOND EDITION, REVISED

METHUEN & CO. LTD. LONDON
36 Essex Street, Strand, W.C.2

First published June 16th 1921
Second edition, revised, 1947

CATALOGUE NO. 3699/U

PRINTED IN GREAT BRITAIN

PREFACE

THIS little book is intended not so much for the student of psychology as for the ordinary man. It is true it has been written partly with the purpose of meeting the needs of W.E.A. classes and courses for social study, such as the classes the writer has himself had experience of teaching in Edinburgh. But, while the needs of such readers have been kept in view throughout, an attempt has also been made to present the matter in a way that would interest and assist the intelligent man in the street who desires to know something of what has been done by the psychologist in this new field. Much psychological activity has been recently manifested in this field of industry and commerce, and it has indeed become imperative that the results should be known to a wider public. That may be taken as the main object of the present work.

There are several books in existence, especially by American writers, which profess the same object. Nevertheless there seems to be room for a book adhering more to the psychological point of view, and emphasizing principles rather than details or results to a greater extent than most of the existing books. In the works of the scientific-management engineers, while there is much lip-service to psychology, the psychology itself is with difficulty recognizable by the professed psychologist. Even in the works of psychologists there is a marked tendency to stress results, and to overlay the discussion with so many illustrations drawn from practical life, that the general lines of the underlying psychology are apt to be obscured. It is all the more necessary to present the psychology as a definite and more or less coherent system because of the fact that the ordinary man has a somewhat distorted view regarding the nature of the science. The writer on a recent occasion lectured in a Scottish manufacturing town on some of the developments of applied psychology, and learned afterwards that one of the criticisms passed on the lecture by an intelligent working man was that 'it was not psychology, but common sense'. Such a criticism encourages the writer in believing that a clear exposition of the applied psychology of industry and commerce will appeal to the practical man as at bottom 'common sense'.

Another recent conversation with a working man, that deeply impressed the writer, was with an intelligent miner, a travelling companion in a railway carriage. He began from the position that it was our scientists who had enabled us to win the war, and he developed a line of argument practically identical with that in Chapters II and III of the present work. It seemed to the writer that the refutation of the statement that the working man was hostile to the application of psychology in industry was as complete as it well could be. The working man is naturally hostile to what he considers exploitation at the hands of the capitalist, but an honest investigation of the facts, and a courageous following in practice of the conclusions to which such an investigation leads, will always have the strongest kind of appeal for him.

It is incumbent on the psychologist discussing industrial problems to observe scrupulously the frontiers of his science. As a psychologist he is concerned with facts, and is strictly impartial towards the claims of capital and labour, so far as these involve questions of policy and rights. Of course even the psychologist may express an opinion on policy—will almost certainly be led to do so by his study of the facts— but he must make it quite clear that in doing so he is no longer speaking as a psychologist, but as a social philosopher or a citizen. It is a profound error for the psychologist to put forward as a psychological principle what is ethics, or politics, or social philosophy, or even religion. First, last, and always, the duty of the psychologist is to study his facts, and to formulate the laws expressing the causal sequence and interdependence of these facts. At that point his duty as a psychologist ends; if he goes further he must speak as a political or social philosopher, or reformer, not as a psychologist.

The author desires specially to acknowledge his indebtedness for underlying principles to Professor McDougall, and for illustrations to Münsterberg, Hollingworth, Muscio, and Myers.

J. D.

UNIVERSITY OF EDINBURGH
January 1921

PREFATORY NOTE TO THE SECOND EDITION

IN the present edition the aim, as before, has been to emphasize principles, rather than details, to bring out, perhaps even more clearly, the relation of psychology to economics, and of education to industry. Stress is also laid on the new urgency which the Second World War has given to many of the problems discussed. Finally, to an even greater extent than previously, the appeal is to the general reader, rather than the specialist in either economics or psychology.

J. D.

EDINBURGH
February 1946

CONTENTS

APPENDICES

CHAPTER I

INTRODUCTION

THE most striking characteristic of the history of the last century is the great progress made by science, and the marvellous changes effected on social and industrial life, as a consequence direct or indirect of this progress. If we may specify at all, we may say that there are two spheres of human activity in particular in which these changes are specially noticeable—the practice of medicine and the manufacture of commodities. But it is also a notable fact that the most important element in all human activity, the human element itself—human nature, to use the popular phrase—is precisely the element which has until recently been most neglected in the advance of science and applied science, and especially in both these spheres. Let us limit our view to industrial and commercial life. At every point in the manufacture, handling, and transportation of goods, we can see the results of applied science; similarly in the market, the shop, the office, inventions which facilitate economically important processes meet the eye on every side. Science does not stop at the concrete and the material. There is a science which investigates the laws of the production, distribution, and exchange of commodities—the science of economics—and the principles of that science are also in a measure recognized and consciously applied in modern commercial and industrial life. Yet, it must be repeated, the most important factor of all is the factor which has hitherto been most neglected in the application of science to modern life—the factor studied by the science of psychology.

A recent writer has remarked, somewhat paradoxically, that psychology is a very old science, but it has a very short history. Like most paradoxes the statement contains only that bit of truth it is intended to call attention to. As a science in the strict sense, psychology is not old. The earliest systems of thought, the germ from which have developed modern science and modern philosophy, may be said to have been reared under the influence of two main motives: (1) the desire to gain control over natural processes, in order to satisfy needs and attain ends, and (2) a restless craving to penetrate into the secrets of the universe for the mere satisfaction of knowing and understanding. The second motive would naturally be characteristic only of a few individuals in any community. These became the philosophers of the early civilization. While the science of the practical man, motived by the first of these motives, was in embryo, imposing systems of speculative philosophy were built up.

We may take this to be the radical distinction between speculative philosophy and science: that the final court of appeal for science is the world of fact and practical applicability to the world of fact, that it studies actual happenings with a perfectly neutral or open mind, allowing the facts themselves to suggest and to test the theories by which an attempt is made to present them in orderly sequence and mutual interdependence; while, on the other hand, the final court of appeal for speculative philosophy is the rational, and it applies its theories to the world of fact with the presupposition that this world is a rational world. Under the conditions of primitive life the practical motive and the practical criteria would obviously not carry men very far in the direction of scientific knowledge. Hence, as we have seen, at the beginning speculative philosophy got a long start of positive science.

Now from very early times speculative philosophy has been greatly interested in that very group of phenomena which constitutes the special province of the science of psychology as we understand it. Thoughts, feelings, desires, emotions, were looked upon as manifestations of the mind or soul, a substance quite distinct from the matter of which external bodies consisted. Many of the deepest and most momentous problems were raised by the relation of this mind and this matter to one another. Hence one of the chief interests of philosophers came to be to interpret both in such a way as to satisfy the demands of the human reason, on the one hand, and the needs of the human spirit, on the other. Thus was created the atmosphere in which the 'old' psychology came into being. It was characteristic of this 'old' psychology that it was either deduced from the supposed nature of the mind or soul, or it was formed by the observation and selection of those facts of experience and consciousness which seemed to support a certain view of the nature of the mind or soul, or it was reached partly in the one way, partly in the other. In any case the 'old' psychology could not in strictness be described as a science. It was the battleground of contending philosophical systems. The truths generally accepted as established principles were submerged in the vast mass of controversial matter, in regard to which some held one opinion, some another, according to the philosophical views which required to be supported. As a result the interminable disputes obscured the very real advances in psychological knowledge that were made. Such was, without any exaggeration, the position of psychology from the time of Plato and Aristotle, or even earlier, till the eighteenth or nineteenth century. As a science it had practically no history during that period.

In the meantime very important events were taking place in the domain of positive science. As civilization developed life became more and more complex. As life became more complex its practical needs multiplied. Under the stimulus of these needs knowledge of, and control over, natural phenomena rapidly extended. This is not the place to trace in detail the development of positive science. Suffice it to say that the application of the method of science led to triumphs in one field after another. It was inevitable that sooner or later the method of science would be applied in the field of psychology also, and indeed to every problem where the conclusions of philosophy come into contact with the world of fact. It is the application of the method of science in the field of mental phenomena that has given us the modern science of psychology—the so-called 'new' psychology.

It is perhaps worth while indicating briefly what the change from the 'old' psychology to the 'new' really amounts to. This is best done by taking the definition of the science from the respective points of view. The 'old' definition of psychology was 'the science of the mind or soul', or 'the science of mental or conscious processes'. The 'new' definition of psychology is 'the science of the facts of human nature and human behaviour', or 'the science of human behaviour in its relation to, and dependence upon, mental process'. There is indeed a strong body of opinion among present-day psychologists in favour of defining psychology simply in terms of behaviour. In any case the tendency is always to lay stress upon the actual facts studied, and by preference the objective facts. The 'new' psychologist rightly holds that to define his science in terms of mind or soul is to define it in terms not of facts, but of an inference from facts which might be challenged, and is therefore entirely illegitimate as a basis for such definition.

This 'new' psychology really made a serious start with the application of experimental methods some seventy years ago. A quarter of a century later, when experimental psychology had already made substantial progress, systematic efforts were begun to develop applied psychology in various fields. This was an inevitable outcome of the change in attitude and point of view. In all respects, therefore, the history of the science has been that of the other sciences from the time when it first took shape as a definite science. One of the main purposes of the present work is to indicate the results of some of these efforts to build up an applied psychology. We may take these results as evidence of the extent to which psychology is already prepared to meet its obligations to practical life.

A word with respect to the point of view of applied psychology will not be out of place. As a science of facts it is not concerned with the advocating of any policy, educational, economic, or political. The ends which are to be attained, the results which it is desirable to produce, are settled independently of psychology. The concern of that science, as applied, is merely the best way in which these ends can be attained, or these results produced. Hence psychology is neither unionist nor radical, neither protectionist nor free-trade, neither capitalist nor labourist, neither individualist nor communist. The claims of each or any of these political, economic, or social philosophies are entirely outside the province of psychology; all that psychology has to discuss is the way in which, having regard to the facts, any particular line of policy may be best pursued, and the psychological results which will follow—not in the slightest degree the merits or demerits of the line of policy itself, except so far as the policy seeks to attain ends which are psychologically impossible with the means to hand.

Apart from this general standpoint, which is characteristic of all sciences, pure and applied alike, applied psychology may be said to differ somewhat from pure psychology in the point where it lays its emphasis. Pure psychology seeks to understand the behaviour of living organisms, and especially of human beings, by understanding the mental processes, the thoughts, feelings, desires, and purposes, which underlie the behaviour. But applied psychology seeks to go beyond the mere understanding. It seeks not only, and not mainly, to understand behaviour and mental process, but to use such insight as we possess, or can gain, in guiding behaviour in a definite direction, and towards the production of definite results. Consequently applied psychology lays far more stress on external results. It is, as we say, predominantly objective. Further, it is less concerned with general laws and principles, more with the individual human being in the concrete, and the correlation of his nature and behaviour with the concrete claims and needs of practical life.

As our aim is to consider applied psychology in the economic sphere, it is also necessary to be clear as regards its relation to economics. Marshall defines economics as 'a study of man's actions in the ordinary business of life'.[1] This is interesting and curious because it is almost exactly how a behaviourist might describe human psychology. Nothing could show more clearly how close the two sciences

[1] *Economics of Industry*, p. 1.

can come to each other, when we consider the relation of both to ordinary life. If, again, we define economics as the science which studies the activities of human society involved in the production, distribution, and exchange of commodities, we still experience difficulty in marking off its proper field from that of psychology. The activities of society are the activities of individual members of society, which find their motive and explanation in the underlying mental processes of individual human beings. The truth is we can only separate the field of economics from the field of psychology by recognizing that economics is really an abstract science, which deals with one aspect only of the activities of the human being or of human society—the economic aspect— and that we obtain the economic aspect by ruling out that part of the concrete fact in which the psychologist is interested, by assuming a society consisting of standard economic individuals, not the concrete human society which is the primary fact. Psychology might indeed be said to take up the investigation of the activities of human society at the point at which economics, as it were, leaves off, by studying the concrete activities of the concrete individuals.

Ruskin, it will be remembered, made some violent attacks on the science of economics and those who pursued it.[1] The attacks were of course quite wrongly directed. We might as well attack the hosiery manufacturer because we cannot get a supply of boots and shoes in his warehouse, as attack the economist because he gives us no account of the altruistic side of human nature. The economist does not profess to supply the goods. That is the business, or part of the business, of the psychologist. All the same, Ruskin's contention and criticisms appear to be valid against economists who claim to apply their findings directly to social activities in the concrete, irrespective of the nature and behaviour of the concrete individual, as economists have on occasion tried to do. Taking for a moment the wider point of view which Ruskin takes, we may hold that the factors which economics does not investigate, which it, as it were, takes for granted, are

[1] See, for example, *Unto this Last.*

precisely the factors which in the world of concrete reality give meaning and significance to every economic process, which underlie and maintain all economic activity. Human needs, impulses, and desires constitute the very driving force of economic life. The processes in the economic world are each and all inspired by human purposes, carried through by human labour, ingenuity, and skill. When we speak of economic forces we are speaking abstractly. In strictness there are no separate economic forces. We so designate from our abstract point of view forces which are really either physical or psychological. In all the applied social sciences the problems are psychological as well as economic, and the fundamental problems being human problems are primarily psychological rather than economic.

While economist and industrialist—labourist as well as capitalist—would probably be prepared to admit all this when advanced as a theoretical position, in nine cases out of ten they would argue that it was after all merely a pious opinion, and that practically the science of psychology was not in a position to yield any significant assistance in the solving of the various industrial problems of modern life, whereas the science of economics was in such a position. The argument would have been perfectly sound twenty years ago. In a measure it is perhaps still sound up to a point. Nevertheless it is possible to show that psychology promises that it will soon be, if it is not already, in a position to perform practically many of the services which ought theoretically to be performed by that science. It is certain that there have been notable developments of recent years, more particularly in social psychology, and in certain branches of applied psychology, which ought to change the whole attitude towards psychology of economist, industrialist, and social reformer. Social psychology will only be touched upon in a cursory way in what follows. Our main concern is applied psychology in the sphere of industry and commerce. It must be clearly understood, however, that this is only one direction in which the results of modern psychology are relevant to problems of social and economic life.

What we may describe as psychological problems of the economic life arrange themselves in three well-marked groups: (1) Problems of the worker—his character, intelligence, vocational fitness and the like; (2) Problems of the work, and the factors upon which its efficiency depends, such as fatigue, length of work and rest periods, economy of movement, conditions of working, and the like; (3) Problems of the market, that is, of demand and supply from the psychological point of view.

Within recent times a definite branch of applied psychology, calling itself 'industrial psychology', has sprung up. The first two groups of problems are its recognized subject-matter, and it might be defined in terms of this subject-matter. It may, however, be defined in such a way as to bring out still more clearly its relation to economics. As a recent writer expresses it, 'all that the application of psychology to industry means essentially is that the aim of industry, whatever this is, may be effected more easily' as a consequence of the utilizing of psychological knowledge.[1] This implies that industrial psychology aims at the elimination of waste—economic and consequent social waste—in so far as it can help in this elimination. We can therefore say that 'industrial psychology' is the utilizing of psychological knowledge (1) in selecting workers for any work on the basis of natural fitness, and (2) in developing good methods of work, in order that a given expenditure of human energy may yield a maximum result, or, which amounts to the same thing, that the result which must be produced may be produced in the most economical way as far as expenditure of human energy is concerned. We would, however, interpret the psychology of industry somewhat more widely than this, so as to include at least the third group of problems, and to include also some reference to the more general psychological conditions affecting industry, as not merely an economic, but also a social, activity.

One other preliminary point requires to be noted. That is the relation of 'industrial psychology' or the wider psychology of industry to that 'scientific management' which since the

[1] Muscio, *Lectures in Industrial Psychology*.

beginning of the present century has become so prominent a feature of American industrial life. The aim of 'scientific management' is confessedly to increase output and profits, and it approaches the psychological phenomena of industrial activities from the point of view of the management. It has naturally been regarded with grave suspicion by the worker from the outset. It may be true that, theoretically and in the long run, the interests of employer and employee coincide. It is none the less true that practically the employee may be exploited for the immediate benefit of the employer. 'Scientific management' makes only a half-hearted profession of impartiality in this matter. Industrial psychology, on the other hand, is strictly impartial, as we have already pointed out. It is concerned solely with the facts, and its investigations and results are equally at the service of both employer and employee. On the whole its tendency has perhaps been to support the worker and his claims, since the worker is the effective agent in nearly every process it investigates, and an understanding of the facts is impossible without understanding the point of view of the worker, as well as the psychological processes involved in the work itself. The industrial psychologist is tempted to reply to the contention of the advocates of scientific management, that efficiency in production is in the interests of the worker as well as the employer, with the equally valid contention that the welfare of the worker is essential to efficient production and to the prosperity and happiness of the community.

CHAPTER II

THE MENTAL CAPITAL OF A NATION

BY far the most important part of the wealth of a nation is what economists call the immaterial part—the character, capacities, aptitudes, and skills of the individual citizens. This, with the physical well-being, has sometimes been spoken of as 'the self-dependent power of a nation'. When engaged in industrial and economic activities, in the widest sense, we may speak of this as the nation's mental capital. In the past far too little attention has been given by economists and others to the distribution of this capital—in the statistical sense of distribution, not the economic—as well as to its most effective utilization, which must be regarded as the main theme of a psychology of industry.

Consider the distribution in the community—our own or any civilized community—of general mental capacity, or what is usually spoken of as general intelligence. In 1932 the Scottish Council for Research in Education carried out an important investigation,[1] widely known as 'the Scottish Mental Survey of 1932', in which every child born in Scotland in the year 1921 was given an intelligence test. It was assumed that the testing of a whole year group would give a fairly accurate indication of the distribution of mental capacity in the nation as a whole. The actual distribution found conformed closely, as expected, to what is known as 'normal frequency distribution'. That is to say, when the distribution was plotted as a curve it took the form shown in the accompanying figure, where the mental level, as given by the score is measured along OX, and the frequency of each level by the height above OX, that is along OY, M representing the mean or median score. The importance of this lies in the fact that the mathematical properties of this curve are known, and tables have been prepared by means

---

[1] *The Intelligence of Scottish Children*, Lond. Univ. Press, 1932.

of which the relative frequency of any score represented by a point along OX can be immediately read off, provided we know the 'scatter', measured by what is known as the 'standard deviation' of the scores, which we can, of course, obtain from the scores themselves.

The importance of this is far greater than is apparent to the man in the street, and it is important both for education and for industry. Here we have, as it were, a law of nature, in accordance with which the mental capacity, from the

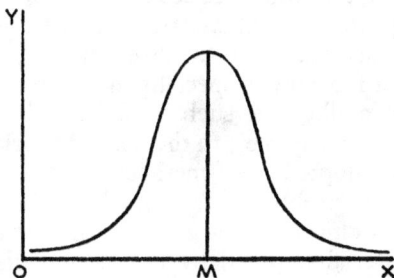

point of view of education, and the mental capital, from the point of view of industry, of the nation is distributed, and no action on the part of the sovereign power, whatever form that may take—dictatorship, aristocracy, democracy, or communism—can alter the law. Educationally the mode in which mental capacity is distributed determines, or ought to determine, the educational provision made in the different grades of educational institution for the different grades of mental capacity, if the nation is to be able to avail itself, to the full, of such mental capacity. Industrially the amount and distribution of mental capital is obviously no less important. If industry requires for certain tasks high mental capacity, then the available capacity of the required level may be so limited in the nation at large, that its fullest possible conservation may become imperative.

The history of intelligence testing and personnel selection in the two World Wars is full of lessons in this connexion. In the call-up of an age group in this country, let us suppose that 250,000 men altogether are contained in this group. Assuming that they may be taken as a representative sample of the total male population, less than 25,000 of them will have a mental level 25 per cent above the level of the average member of the community. Actually the number available for service will be considerably less in the case of the higher age groups, since many of the men of high capacity will already be in positions of such responsibility that they will not be called up, and of those called up some at least will be physically unfit, and will be rejected on that or other ground. From the top 10 per cent must be supplied practically all the commissioned officers in the three services, together with those required for various specialist duties which demand a high level of intelligence, such as fighter pilots or bomber observers in the Air Force. In the Second World War, when this country adopted test methods in the selection of personnel, acute problems were found to arise with respect particularly to officer shortage, from this limitation of the necessary material imposed by the natural distribution of that material in the community.

In peace-time, as in war-time, this limitation of our human resources must be kept clearly in view. Its significance is not merely military. Every branch of the economic and industrial activity of a community is obviously affected by this limitation. This fact, that mental capacity is distributed in a certain way in the community, is a basal fact from the point of view of the economic and industrial efficiency of the community. Not only are there certain economic tasks which require for their efficient performance a high mental capacity, and which cannot otherwise be efficiently performed, but all economic tasks require for their efficient performance a certain minimal level of capacity, and a certain easily calculable proportion of the community will be below that level. Moreover it is economically wasteful, and possibly to a serious extent, to employ a high level of capacity for a task for which a much lower level is quite adequate, and clearly all the more serious since the higher the level the more limited is the available supply.

So far the community point of view has been emphasized. From the individual point of view there are equally important considerations to be kept in mind. An individual worker who is faced with a task for which his capacity is barely adequate, or even totally inadequate, cannot possibly be contented and happy in his employment. He is a definite misfit, not because he is a square peg in a round hole, but because he is a small peg in a large hole. At best he is bound to be inefficient, but his own sense of inadequacy will tend to increase his inefficiency, even if more serious results to his mental stability do not show themselves. On the other hand, an individual who is kept working at tasks far below his real capacity can hardly be expected to take much interest in his work, and may become in consequence less efficient than would be an individual of a much lower capacity. A large peg in a small hole, he can hardly fail to become socially inefficient as well, and possibly in extreme cases a social handicap, if not menace.

There is current a vague popular notion, possibly the outcome of a kind of wishful thinking, that inequalities of capacity can be largely smoothed out by education. They can to a certain extent, but any smoothing out will be downwards, and not upwards. The school can do much to promote social and economic efficiency, but it cannot increase natural capacity, and education is itself subject to the same limitations we are considering. There are educational issues involved in this connexion, which are so vitally important for the industrial life and efficiency of the community, that some further attention must be devoted to them. They may be primarily educational issues, but they are also vital industrial issues. In a democratic community the mental level of the child ought clearly to be one of the main determining factors with respect to the kind and range of the education he receives. It is also obviously one important determining factor with respect to the nature of the economic service he is capable of rendering. Hence, from the point of view of national economy and industrial efficiency, it is of the utmost importance that school education and industrial, or, more generally, economic, service should be so dovetailed into one another, if one may so speak, as to allow of the minimum of capacity wastage. To some extent the new Education Acts of both England and Scotland have this point in view, but educational thought in this country is still to a large extent dominated by those 'culture' and 'leisure' ideals and ends of education, which hark back to Ancient Greece and a fallacious interpretation of the teaching of Aristotle.

The immensity of the gulf, which separates the social and economic life of to-day from the social and economic life of Ancient Greece, is only too apt to be forgotten in our enthusiasm for the kind of culture, and the liberal education, which the Greeks developed. Greek civilization was a civilization served by slave labour. The social efficiency of the Greek, or more particularly the Athenian, citizen was divorced from economic efficiency to an extent that has become impossible, even if desirable, in the great development of industrial and commercial activity, and the free labour, of the modern world.

All this may seem irrelevant to a discussion of the psychology of industry, but it is really closely relevant. The education of a community cannot, without serious dangers, be divorced from the economic life of the community. The persistence in our schools and universities of the ideals and attitudes of an alien culture is actually one of the most serious handicaps under which the economic and industrial development of our day labours, and all the more serious because of the pervasiveness and subtlety of their influence. Here are some interesting figures from Scotland, where, thanks to the work of the Research Council and the Scottish Education Department, we are able, to some extent, to trace what is happening. The number of pupils completing their primary or elementary education, and fitted on the basis of their mental level for a five years' secondary course, was in 1929 about 24,000. In the following year (1930) 30,700 began such a course in secondary schools. In 1931 the number had dropped to 22,000, in 1932 to 14,000, in 1933 to 7,400, in 1934 to 5,000. In 1934 the number obtaining their leaving certificate, and presumably qualified to enter on a university course, was 3,650. The number actually entering the universities was 1,500. Of this age group the number fitted by mental level to enter upon university study, professional, technological, commercial, or general, according to reasonable standards based on the Scottish Survey, was about 9,000.[1]

While it must be admitted that these figures represent the resultant of a great variety of complex conditions and factors, they show unmistakably that our secondary schools and our universities are not playing the part they might play in the economic life of the community, that young people are filtering into industrial, commercial, and possibly domestic employments without reaching that level of educational preparation for which their mental level fits them, and in some cases long before they have reached that level of preparation which it is obviously in the interest of the community that they should attain. It may be suggested that this is in part due to the fact that the education they are receiving in the secondary school, or will receive in the university, is felt by them, or their parents, or both, to have little significance for the practical life which calls them. This suggestion is in some degree supported by the general attitude of the leaders of industry and commerce towards the university man.

The position in England is, if anything, worse, since a much smaller proportion of the population enter the universities. In both countries the only socially and economically important function of the universities is as professional schools, and this function they perform almost accidentally. All the time, especially in the older universities, many voices are heard proclaiming that the real function of a university is to prepare for a life of research and contemplation, or, as far as the Arts Faculty in particular is concerned, to give a 'liberal education' in the sense in which that was understood by Aristotle, wholly oblivious of the fact that an education which leaves one unable to share in, or even to appreciate and

[1] The educational implications the author means to discuss elsewhere.

understand, the social and economic movements characteristic of the civilization of the modern world is thoroughly illiberal.

The fact is we must re-define such words as 'liberal', 'culture', 'leisure' in terms of twentieth-century Western civilization. 'Leisure' has already been re-defined, but in such a way that the implications of the word in relation to the life of the time are essentially different from its implications in the mind of Aristotle. 'Leisure' with us carries with it the notion of recreation, and recreation inevitably suggests the pre-existence of serious activity, after which some restoration of physical or mental energy and tone is required. In addition, of course, to this notion of recreation, there is the further suggestion of activities that are for the individual worth-while activities, which latter is more in accordance with Aristotle's meaning. It is a short step, but still in consonance with Aristotle's thought to the position that the day's work is to be regarded as more or less servile— 'banausic' to use the Greek adjective in English guise. The psychological effect of any such attitude can only be regarded as highly unfortunate.

This seeming digression has led us to issues which appear primarily to be the concern of the social philosopher, and which may be left to him at the point we have reached. For us the important points are two: in the first place, the fact that school and university, as well as industry, have to take account of the limitations arising from the distribution in the community of mental capacity, and, in the second place, that the education given in our secondary schools and universities, the education presumably, therefore, of children and youths of the higher grades of capacity, is largely divorced from the economic life of the community. The importance of this second fact will become clearer and clearer as we proceed, and the demand that something be done about it will find stronger and stronger justification.

Perhaps the most convincing evidence of the part played by capacity distribution, under conditions approximating in complexity the conditions in the industrial world, is the actual personnel distribution, worked out by psychologists in this country and in America, for various units organized in the battalions and regiments composing an army. This distribution was based, on the one hand, on the capacities and aptitudes of the individual men, and, on the other hand, on the kind of duties to be performed in the units in question under service conditions. The initial distribution was on the basis of mental level as determined by preliminary testing. By this preliminary testing the men were graded into, let us say, seven grades. The figures given in illustration below are hypothetical—the actual figures are confidential. The distribution in, let us suppose, an armoured car regiment would work out in some such way as this: no man of the lowest two grades would be posted, 4 per cent of the regiment could be assigned duties that could be performed by the fifth grade, 70 per cent would have to perform duties requiring the third or fourth grade in about equal numbers, about 20 per cent would have to be assigned duties requiring second-grade level, and the rest would have to be of the highest grade—6 per cent.

Is this not closely analogous to the position that must arise in the case of any large factory, or, more generally, when industry as a whole is to be organized, in order to attain the highest efficiency? There are industrial tasks which demand the highest grade of mental capacity, and there are industrial tasks which can be performed by individuals of a much lower grade. There are intermediate tasks suitable for intermediate grades. In economic life as a whole the grade distribution must more or less closely correspond to the grade distribution in the community at large. Only by selecting, training, and placing its personnel on this basis can industry make the fullest use of the mental capacity available in the community, and the nation at large, by acting on the same lines, make the fullest use of its mental capital.

The general mental level of an individual is probably the most important factor determining the grade of industrial, as of educational, activity, which he is capable of undertaking. There are, however, other factors, congenital or acquired, which must also be taken into account. There are special aptitudes, distributed for the most part, if congenital, in the same way as general capacity, and these special aptitudes adapt individuals for specific kinds of industrial or commercial activity. There are physical and temperamental characteristics, some of which may be of high significance with reference to particular types of industrial or commercial occupation. All these factors, which appear to present the first and the most fundamental problems for a psychology of industry, will receive attention in the chapters which follow.

CHAPTER III

GENERAL CAPACITY AND SPECIAL APTITUDES

THE differences between human beings and the practical importance of these differences may be said to have been already recognized long before a systematic psychology came upon the scene. Such pseudo-sciences as palmistry, physiognomy, and phrenology owed most of their one-time popularity to their claims that they could throw light on an individual's abilities and aptitudes. The systematic study of these differences began with the work of Francis Galton. In 1869, in his *Hereditary Genius*, he described how a scale might be constructed, so that men might be classified according to their natural endowments. Galton's interest, however, was theoretical rather than practical. The practical development, which has to-day attained such wide extension, and such magnitude, really began with the work of Binet in France, though McKeen Cattell in America and Kraepelin in Germany had already indicated possible lines of practical development.

Binet's earliest work in the field of mental testing, which appeared in *L'Annee Psychologique* in 1895, was more or less on the same lines as the work of Galton and Cattell, but in 1904 he was invited to solve a practical problem in connexion with the selection for special instruction of backward children in the Paris schools. This determined the main line of his subsequent work, and initiated one of the most significant psychological and educational developments of our time. His aim now came to be to devise a scale by means of which it would be possible to measure, as with a kind of measuring-rod, the mental level reached by the individual child.

In 1905, 1908, and 1911 Binet gave to the world three such mental measuring-rods. In all three cases tests of the same general type were employed, and in all three cases these tests were arranged in order of increasing difficulty. The tests also were themselves all of a relatively simple nature, requiring no elaborate apparatus, and involving only such knowledge and information as an individual might reasonably be expected to acquire in the ordinary intercourse of everyday life, independently of what is normally acquired through schooling. The scales of 1908 and 1911 showed one important change, as compared with that of 1905; the tests were arranged in age groups, not in a continuous series. These scales have formed the basis or model of almost all later developments in individual testing, and most scales subsequently devised have been either modifications or imitations of the Binet scales.

The modifications of the Binet scale which have been most widely used are those due mainly to Terman, and known as the Stanford Revision and the Terman-Merrill Revision respectively. Both attempt to correct defects in the original scale, and the latter may be said to represent the most elaborate, most extensive, and possibly the most perfect measuring instrument of this kind at present available, though it has not yet wholly superseded the older Stanford Revision in general use. To obtain a measurement of mental level with either of these scales all that is necessary is to find the point beyond which the individual is unable to pass any further test, take the last age group where he has been successful in all the tests, add to the corresponding age one, two, or more months, according to the part of the scale reached, for every success beyond that age. We thus obtain what is called the mental age (M.A.) of the individual, from which we can, if necessary, ascertain what is called the intelligence quotient (I.Q.), which is the ratio of mental age to chronological age, expressed as a percentage of average level, which is correspondence of the two—M.A. and C.A.

Binet, we have said, sought to devise tests which would be independent of schooling. He was not wholly successful. It has been shown that children with a minimum of schooling, or none at all, are placed much lower by the scale than they really are, judged by all other indications. This holds, not only of the Binet scales, but of all scales based on the Binet, or similar to the Binet. In view of this fact, and other facts to which reference will be made presently, many psychologists hold that scales of the Binet type should always be supplemented by what are called 'performance tests', if we wish to get a true rendering of a child's level, and this is particularly essential where important decisions hinge on the results of the testing.

The characteristic difference between the Binet type of test and a performance test lies in the fact that the Binet type is in general of the question and answer kind and highly verbal, while in the performance test the individual is asked to do something, involving handling concrete material, rather than to say something. The relative merits of the two types of test need not delay us here. It is at least certain, however, that the performance test, with its emphasis on the handling of objects, has a different kind of appeal to the subject, and affords an opportunity of assessing an aspect of intelligent behaviour which is not unimportant from a practical point of view. The verbal nature of the Binet type of test also undoubtedly increases the possibility of a bias being given to the results in one direction by the higher educational attainments of a subject, or in the opposite direction by any language defect or any defect of hearing.

Up to the time of the First World War the practical use of mental tests was confined mainly to school children and individual tests were normally those employed. But the study of theoretical problems by means of mental tests had been developed to a considerable extent, and in such study group methods were often employed. This had resulted in the devising of the type of test called the 'group test', tests of the Binet type being quite inapplicable. The first extensive use of group tests for practical, as distinct from theoretical, purposes came with the entry of America into the war. Individual testing is admittedly more accurate, and more satisfactory from almost every point of view. Its one serious disadvantage is the time it takes. It also requires expert handling. When large numbers have to be tested, and both time and testing personnel are limited, individual testing must be abandoned, and group testing must take its place.

Already before the First World War American psychologists had become awake to the possibilities of testing on a large scale by using the group methods, developed for the study of theoretical problems by Spearman in England and by Thorndike in America. Some Americans, such as Otis, had already gone so far as to prepare the necessary test material. Confidence in the usefulness of mental tests was already in America such that, when Robert M. Yerkes, at that time President of the American Psychological Association, set to work to organize a team of psychologists to develop tests for the testing of all men called to the colours in America, the value and significance of ascertaining by means of tests the mental level of these men, with a view to their being utilized to the best advantage in the great army which was being built up, was at once realized.

Group tests were prepared—six equivalent series in all— and arrangements were made to test the army recruits in large groups. Provision was also made for the testing of illiterates and those immigrants whose knowledge of the English language was inadequate, by series of more or less equivalent non-verbal tests. Methods of grading the men on the basis of the test results were devised, normal frequency distribution being assumed. In doubtful cases, and for all men graded in the lowest category, arrangements were made for supplementing the group tests by recognized individual tests, while tests were also devised for assessing special capacities requisite in special branches of the service.

The marked success which attended the employment of these American Army tests may be said to have initiated a new large-scale movement and opened a new chapter in the history of mental testing. One American psychologist, writing of the testing, and the results achieved, says: 'If some other country with more permanent policies should take up the mental analyses where we have left them, and develop a real military psychology, they would have a military instrument vastly more effective than 42 cm. guns.'

Germany did exactly this, developing and maintaining a highly organized psychological branch of the German army, the effects of which were clearly visible in the first two or three years of the Second World War.

But this military development was by no means the only sequel to the American Army testing. An ever-widening employment of group tests for educational purposes in the first instance, and later for industrial purposes as well, followed immediately on the conclusion of the armistice, not confined to America, though initiated there, but spreading quickly to other countries, until the group mental test became a quite normal adjunct to the ordinary entrance examination for schools of all grades, and in America for colleges and universities, while many large industrial undertakings, again mainly in America, added the group test to their methods of selecting employees.

The general principles underlying the construction of group tests are similar to those for individual tests. Mental tasks of different kinds are presented, so as to test a variety of aspects of the individual's mental capacity or ability. These tasks are arranged roughly in order of increasing difficulty in booklets. Each individual is supplied with a booklet, together with a pencil. Various devices are employed to make the answering of the questions, and the scoring of the answers as easy and expeditious as possible. The booklet of tests may be arranged on either of two principles. All the questions or tasks of the same type are kept together—the 'battery' type—or the tasks are varied, a group of four or five of one type being succeeded by a group of four or five of another type, that by a group of a third kind, and so on, the succession being repeated until all the tests have been used—the 'omnibus' type. In the 'battery' type each series of tasks must be timed separately; in the 'omnibus' type there is only one timing for the whole. Each method has its advantage. In the First World War the American Army tests were of the 'battery' type, in the Second the 'omnibus' type was preferred.

There is considerable difference of opinion among

psychologists as to the degree of accuracy to be expected of measurement by means of group tests. It is generally agreed, however, that their accuracy is inferior to that of the recognized individual tests, and where important issues depend on the test results, individual tests of the Binet type, possibly with the addition of performance tests, should always be used, if practicable. Apart, however, from 'accuracy', by which we mean fineness of discrimination, there are at least two other characteristics, which satisfactory mental tests, individual and group alike, must possess, before we can use them with any degree of confidence. The first of these is what is usually called 'reliability' or 'consistency'. That is to say, they must yield a relatively constant measurement for the same individual under the same conditions. A measuring rod, which showed irregularity in the measurements obtained, when the conditions were more or less constant, would be of little value as a measuring rod. In the second place they must have the characteristic usually called 'validity'. That is to say, they must measure what we require to measure, and what we assume that they are measuring. Reliability and validity are both essential—the *sine qua non* of mental testing.

The securing of these three characteristics—accuracy, in the sense of fineness of discrimination, reliability, and validity—in the case more particularly perhaps of group tests—sometimes presents problems by no means easy to solve. The main difficulties that arise, and the procedure usually adopted to meet them, may be briefly described. The underlying principles hold of all mental testing. The actual test material to be used, whether arithmetical problems or syllogistic reasoning or following directions, must be graded in order of increasing difficulty, so as to distribute the subjects over the whole range of capacity to be tested. If, for example, in a test using arithmetical problems as the test material, we find fifty per cent of the subjects scoring full points, our test is obviously failing altogether to distribute half our subjects. Similarly, if fifty per cent score no points at all. Generally speaking, we should aim at getting a distribution approximately normal, unless from the nature of the situation that cannot be expected. The practical method of dealing with the situation is to prepare a test that appears adapted to the group to be tested, give it to a group as similar as possible in range and capacity, and on the results, as shown by what is known as the 'answer pattern', that is a table showing the manner in which successes and failures are distributed among the individual items, make any required rearrangement and modifications.

To determine the reliability or consistency of a test the ideal method is to give the test twice, with a suitable interval elapsing, to the same group, and ascertain the extent to which the two results are in agreement. Another easier way, though, theoretically at least, not quite so satisfactory, is to divide the original test into two presumably equivalent tests by taking for each alternate items, give the two tests, so prepared, to the same group, and note as before the extent to which the results are in agreement. In such cases, to get a measure of the degree of agreement what is called the 'reliability coefficient' is calculated.

Most important of all is the validity of a test, and its determination frequently presents the greatest difficulty. In this case as we have seen, we must determine the extent to which the test does what it professes to do, that is, the extent to which it tests what we set out to test. This involves testing or verifying its results by subsequent experience, which may involve a long-delayed validation or the reverse, or alternatively discovering some other criterion and applying that to our test results, which may be exceedingly difficult. Where there is already in existence a test which has been proved to be satisfactory, there is of course little difficulty. In the case of an intelligence test for school children we can obtain an independent criterion from the results of school examinations, or the estimates of the teachers, or a combination of the two. Or, in the case of adults, if we can apply the test to a representative sample of proved capacity, the difficulty is solved. In the case of Service personnel during a war, however, the difficulty becomes very acute. If, for example, we consider the selection of army officers, some considerable time may elapse before any evidence of efficiency under operational conditions is procurable, and a batch of officers tested together may be widely separated before such evidence becomes available at all, so that the collection of data for validation is itself no easy matter, and the data very fragmentary and heterogeneous. Nevertheless some kind of validation is so essential, that all possible efforts should be made to secure it, before the test is employed for any serious practical purpose. In the Scottish Mental Survey of 1932, already referred to, the final validation was obtained in two ways. On the one hand the test was given, under the same conditions as it was to be given in Scotland, to all the children of the same range of age in two English cities, and on the other hand a thousand unselected children, among those tested, or to be tested, by the test, were also tested with the Stanford Revision individual test. The latter procedure not only served to validate the group test, but also made possible the conversion of the group scores into mental ages and intelligence quotients.

Hitherto the discussion has been relevant in the main to the testing of general intelligence or general capacity. It is clear, however, that special capacities may also have special economic and industrial value, and may, no less than general capacity, be made the practical objective in testing. The testing of special capacities is indeed the logical outcome of an applied psychology of individual differences. The industrial and economic significance of differences of special capacities between one man and another were recognized long before the psychologist was in a position to measure such differences, or even dream of the possibility of measuring them. There are gross differences of sensory efficiency, particularly in vision and in hearing, which any comprehensive medical examination will reveal. But in addition to such there are differences in quickness of thought and action, differences in the ability to divide and distribute attention, differences in motor control, differences in learning ability, and many other differences, which may be important in the various industrial tasks of this machine age. For most of these the psychologist is able to devise tests, and some of them he can measure with a high degree of precision. Where such differences are congenital, or have a congenital basis, their distribution, like that of innate general capacity, is in accordance with the normal frequency curve. The same principles, and also the same limitations, are then applicable as have been already discussed. The accuracy, reliability, and validity of the tests employed are equally important, and are determined by the same methods as we use in the case of tests for general capacity. In some cases also group test methods may be used, and in other cases individual methods alone are applicable.

Between one man and another there are also differences which may be termed emotional and temperamental, or differences of feeling and of will, partly congenital, and partly the result of the influence of environmental factors. These, too, are frequently highly significant in industrial life, and highly important from the point of view of industrial efficiency. The assessment and measurement of differences of this kind present entirely new and difficult problems. No reliable method, indeed, of measuring such characteristics has up to the present been evolved. This does not mean that the psychologist is entirely helpless in the face of these problems. A certain measure of assessment of emotional, temperamental, and volitional characteristics may be arrived at by grading methods, rating scales, standardized interview methods, and the like. Such assessment will not give, and cannot be expected to give, that accuracy of discrimination, which tests of intelligence, and of sensory, motor, and intellectual capacities can be made to yield. That must be conceded. They can, however, be developed so as to possess greater reliability and validity than might have been expected.

CHAPTER IV

VOCATIONAL GUIDANCE AND SELECTION

IN recent times a new branch of applied psychology calling itself 'vocational' psychology has come into being, having as its practical aim the solution of the problems for national economy and industrial prosperity raised by the considerations discussed in the last two chapters. Vocational psychology bifurcates normally into the two branches of 'vocational guidance' and 'vocational selection', the former being concerned with the choosing of a vocation or career by the individual, the latter with the choosing of an individual for a particular 'job' or position. In principle there is not so much difference in the psychologist's task between guidance and selection as has sometimes been made to appear. It is true that there is a difference of interest and aim, that in the one case the testing is definitely non-competitive, in the other case tending towards the competitive, that in the one case the result is merely advice, which may or may not be taken, in the other case the result is decision and action. Psychologically, however, these, and most other differences, are largely superficial, or at least not nearly so radical as generally supposed. In the British Army testing during the Second World War the two processes were to a certain extent carried on together, and based on the same test data, at the primary training centres, and in most cases, though not in all, they require the same preliminary investigation, and in the main the same test procedure, on the part of the psychologist. It is convenient to discuss the two separately, but these facts must always be kept in mind.

VOCATIONAL GUIDANCE

Guidance in the choice of an occupation has a twofold importance. From the point of view of the community, it is economically important that its human capital should be employed to the best advantage. It would not be employed to the best advantage if an A-grade man was doing C-grade work, or a C-grade man was making a hopeless mess of A-grade work, or if a man with a special liking and a special aptitude for one kind of work was trying to earn a living in an occupation for which he had neither the taste nor the aptitude. From the point of view of the individual, it is not any less important that he should live a contented and satisfying life, as he could not do if he was maladjusted in his daily work, and the chances of maladjustment are very considerable.

The young person entering on a vocation has obviously little opportunity of gaining a real knowledge of his own special abilities, is often, indeed, not very clear regarding even his own tastes and inclinations. Too often he is guided in his choice of a vocation by what is little more than a mere whim, by imitation of his companions, or by some vague idea that the financial or other prospects in this or that vocation are particularly good. Thus he is led to make one of the most important decisions of his life on grounds that are entirely—sometimes ludicrously, sometimes lamentably —inadequate. He neither knows his own strengths and weaknesses, nor the definite requirements for success in the vocation in question. And when the knowledge comes to him through bitter experience it is often too late. Münsterberg[1] cites in illustration of this the case of a boy with a passion, perhaps real enough, for the life of a sailor, who is quite unfitted for such a life by the fact that he is colour blind, a fact of which he is himself ignorant. The writer has in mind exactly such a case. The boy had been several years at sea and did not realize that his colour vision was defective, until he went up for examination for his second-mate's certificate. The years spent at sea have not only been lost, but have largely unfitted him for other vocations he might have entered five or six years ago. Obviously, as Münsterberg points out, 'similar defects may exist in a boy's attention or memory, judgment or feeling, thought or imagination,

[1] *Psychology and Industrial Efficiency*, Chapter V.

suggestibility or emotion, and they may remain as undiscovered as the defect of colour-blindness'.

To the socially minded the point of view of the community will probably have an even stronger appeal. The most enlightened of the demands for some guidance of the young in the choice of a vocation comes perhaps from the various institutions for social study and social service. These, awake to the social wastage and disaster arising directly out of economic failure, dependent on a wrong initial choice of vocation, everywhere strongly urge the necessity for some adequate scheme of vocational guidance. They tend also to press the apparently very just view that such vocational guidance must be regarded as among the functions and duties of the school authorities, since the school period is *par excellence* the period during which guidance regarding future vocation can be most easily and appropriately given.

The demand was present and articulate long before the psychologist was in a position to attempt to meet it. Before the days of laboratory psychology, indeed, one school of psychology—the phrenologists—acknowledged the duty of the science with respect to this practical demand, and at least deserves the credit of having made an attempt to perform the service. 'I cannot too earnestly repeat', says George Combe, 'that the principles now illustrated are practical and important. If any one require the assistance of a human being, let him be assured that attention to the three elements—of temperament, development of mental organs, and education or training—will afford him more certain information regarding the inherent qualities of the subject and his practical capacities, than certificates of character and attainments such as are commonly relied on.'[1] In fact, take out George Combe's phrenology, and much that he wrote on this subject might be written by a present-day psychologist. Since the failure of the phrenologist many other attempts at vocational diagnosis have been made with foundations even more fantastic.

Scarcely less fantastic were some of the efforts and some

[1] George Combe, *System of Phrenology*, vol. II, p. 318.

of the claims of the earlier advocates of scientific management. Thus Emerson, with the clearest recognition of the problem and its psychological nature,[1] goes so far as to say: 'The competent specialist (psychologist?) who has supplemented natural gifts and good judgment by analysis and synthesis can perceive attitudes and proclivities even in the very young, much more readily in those semi-matured, and can with almost infallible certainty point out, not only what work can be undertaken with fair hope of success, but also what slight modification or addition and diminution will more than double the personal power'.[2] These are simply words concealing the barrenness of his practical ideas on the subject, and attributing to the psychologist powers which at the time he wrote would have been nothing short of miraculous, and which even to-day, with all the progress in accuracy of testing made during recent years, no psychologist of standing would dare to lay claim to—or if he did, would lay himself open to the ridicule of all his psychological colleagues.

The fact is that the problems are fraught with serious difficulties, when a really scientific attempt is made to reach a satisfactory solution. The testing of general and special capacities and aptitudes is now a relatively simple matter, but that will only carry us a part of the way towards a practical solution. Knowledge of the general and special aptitudes required in particular vocations, of the state of the labour market as regards particular vocations, and of the prospects for the future, both for the individual and for the vocation, is also obviously necessary.

In recent years several experiments in vocational guidance have been carried out in Britain. The National Institute of Industrial Psychology carried out the first such experiment in a London borough, and later a second experiment in the county of Fife in Scotland. The propaganda effect of these experiments, and of other efforts on the part of the Institute, led to the appointment in many schools, especially in

[1] He says also for example, in his *Efficiency as a Basis for Operation and Wages*: 'It is psychology, not soil or climate, that enables a man to raise five times as many potatoes per acre as the average in his own state.'
[2] Quoted from Münsterberg, *Psychology and Industrial Efficiency*, p. 53.

England, of 'careers masters', whose function it is to give vocational advice to boys on leaving school, the advice being based partly on school work, partly on the results of testing, partly on the tastes, vocational preferences and the like, of the boys themselves. Actually this is little more than scratching the surface or the real problem. The schools in question are, for the most part, secondary schools (public schools in the English sense), the boys, leaving school at seventeen or eighteen, belong mostly to parents of the well-to-do classes, and are, on the whole, of a relatively high grade of intelligence. The large mass of children in the ordinary schools are untouched, and it does not seem possible to provide for them on the same lines, except at an extravagant cost.

With these considerations in mind, and taking the view already mentioned that vocational guidance is part of the function of education authorities, and should, if possible, be offered to all children leaving school, a Joint Committee of the Edinburgh Education Committee and the Juvenile Employment Committee sanctioned in 1936 an experiment, with the object of testing the practicability of a scheme, by which all children leaving the schools of the Edinburgh Committee might be given vocational advice, without any excessive increase in the cost of education in the city. Unfortunately the follow-up was interrupted by the outbreak of the Second World War, but the procedure adopted appeared to demonstrate the practicability of the scheme, and is therefore worth describing, as indicating the general lines along which any satisfactory solution of the larger problem must be found.

The experiment was put under the direct charge of a research student in the George Combe Psychological Laboratory, working under the general supervision of the Professor of Psychology, and having a group of five or six advanced students attached, to assist in such group testing as was necessary. The subjects were all the pupils in the four largest intermediate schools in the city. These schools provide for the education of pupils from the primary schools, who are not taking the full secondary course up to the Leaving Certificate or University Entrance stage, but a three years' course up to the Day School Certificate stage, that is from age twelve to age fifteen. Since at that time the age of fourteen was the upper limit of the compulsory period, a fair proportion might be expected to leave before the completion of the three years' course was attained. Hence the desirability of testing all the pupils in the schools. There were altogether about three thousand children.

The aim of the experiment, as already indicated, was to devise a scheme of testing which could be carried out by the teaching staff, without any material increase in the personnel, which would not interfere unduly with the ordinary work of the school, which could be completed between the admission of the pupil at age twelve and his leaving at the first leaving date after his attainment of the age of fourteen, and the results of which would supply data upon which vocational advice might, with some degree of confidence, be given to each pupil and his parents, when the actual leaving took place. These conditions limited the kind and scope of the testing that could be undertaken, but it was hoped that the tests would show a degree of validity sufficient to warrant an education committee in putting such a scheme into operation throughout its area. The evidence for validity, as we have seen, was incomplete owing to the outbreak of the war, but the practicability was clearly demonstrated.

The testing procedure could not be wholly stereotyped, since allowance had to be made for varying circumstances and conditions in the different schools. Two questionnaires were filled out for each pupil, one by the parents, the other by the teachers responsible. Each pupil also indicated, on a specially prepared list of occupations, his, or her, preferences for particular occupations in order of preference, first, second, and third. The actual tests employed were: a verbal test of intelligence (Kuhlmann-Anderson, Grade VI, modified), a performance test of intelligence (Moorrees Form-Board, as used in Rowntrees' Cocoa Works at York, reduced to two-thirds size), a mechanical aptitude test (Cox), two manual dexterity tests (nut and bolt and peg-board), and a colour-blindness test (Ishihara). All the tests were given as group tests, the Kuhlmann-Anderson and Cox tests to large groups (one or more classes), the other tests to smaller groups of six to twelve.

On the basis of the results obtained from tests and questionnaires it was possible in most cases to formulate vocational advice of the kind that a scheme of vocational guidance might be expected to yield. At this point, however, an important and often forgotten principle emerges. With relatively rare exceptions, no scheme of vocational guidance will enable us to say that this or that occupation is the one and only occupation for this or that individual. Any claim to do this in every case is the claim of the charlatan. Certain occupations can be definitely excluded, certain others noted as inadvisable, leaving a group of occupations, any one of which may be entered, the ultimate selection depending on the state of the labour market and the preferences of the individual.

That vocational guidance is the function of the school there can be no reasonable doubt. Educational selection as operative in any organized educational system is already in part vocational determination. For example, selecting for secondary education, or for specific courses in the secondary school, is the initiation of guidance of the individual towards certain groups of occupations. Hence a piece of research like that carried out by McClelland[1] in Dundee, under the auspices of the Scottish Research Council and the Scottish Committee of the International Examination Inquiry, is highly relevant to the problems of vocational guidance, while at the same time throwing valuable light on the problems and pitfalls of selection. All educational guidance is indeed already vocational guidance, and the extension of this function of the education committees to advice given to every child leaving school, on choice of vocation, is a natural and inevitable development of the near future. While this is being written a memorandum on the subject has been issued

[1] See *Selecting for Secondary Education*, London Univ. Press.

by the Minister of Labour; it would have come more appropriately from the Minister of Education.

VOCATIONAL SELECTION

While vocational guidance represents an attempt to advise the individual regarding the kind of vocation for which he is best adapted, vocational selection represents an attempt to select the most suitable individual for a particular kind of employment, or, in many cases, for a particular job. The primary concern, in the one case, is the best interest of the would-be employee; in the other case, the best interest of the employer. The two are nevertheless complementary to one another, rather than antagonistic, and adequate service in both respects is in the best interest of the community. Moreover, if vocational guidance is adequately organized in the community, vocational selection by the employer will be greatly facilitated.

In the past the employer has selected his employees in all sorts of ways. In many cases in fact no selection at all has taken place initially; the selection takes place later, as a result of the experience of the employer with regard to the suitability or efficiency of the individual, or the experience of the individual himself with respect to the agreeableness of the work, or the amount of the wages, or the prospects of advancement, or some other, and sometimes highly irrelevant, circumstance. In such cases one may expect a high labour turnover, and where the work is unskilled that may not matter very much. Where any degree of skill is involved, and training is necessary in order to attain efficiency, a high labour turnover will obviously involve considerable economic wastage, since the time spent in training will be lost, in the case of every trained man who leaves, while the time spent in the training of new men, and the inevitable waste of material in the process, will be time and material which might be more profitably utilized.

Where some scheme of selection is in operation—and this is becoming more and more prevalent every day—the basis upon which selection takes place is often totally inadequate, and the wastage due to inefficiency, and a high labour turn-over, is consequently very slightly reduced. Good looks, a pleasing manner, a satisfactory school record, testimonials, written or verbal, from some one acquainted with the applicant for employment, may or may not be of value according to circumstances, the most importance of which is their relevance to the nature of the work to be done, but are very rarely reliable, and most frequently very superficial indicators —like beauty, only skin deep.

Where scientifically based vocational advice has been given an important step has already been taken towards staisfactory selection, but in many undertakings, where high skills, demanding special aptitudes as well as special training, are required, some measures must be taken to secure evidence of the possession of the necessary skills, or aptitudes for acquiring the necessary skills. Hence, even where adequate vocational guidance is provided, there will still be a place for vocational selection in many undertakings. Where such vocational guidance is not provided, the scheme for vocational selection in any undertaking must fill the gap, starting, as it were, from the beginning. There will, however, be one difference. The employer naturally desires to have the best available for his particular purpose. His procedure will therefore be, to use an educational analogy, that of the competitive, rather than the qualifying, examination, which may in some cases radically alter the whole situation. Hence it may be that, in all cases, the employer will prefer to include in his selection procedure most of the lines of investigation, normally followed in vocational guidance, adding the special lines of investigation appropriate to the special kinds of work he has in mind.

The general principles underlying any adequate scheme of vocational selection will already be obvious. The nature and requirements of the general employment, or particular jobs, for which selection is to be made, must be clearly, and even meticulously, appreciated. That is to say, the precise details of the work the individual has to do, and of the calls made on his physical strength and stamina, on his mental capacity, on his mechanical aptitude and skill, on his motor dexterity and control, on his persistence, and generally on the moral and volitional aspects of his personality, must be clearly and fully recognized. This knowledge can hardly be gained from mere external observation: it can only be gained thoroughly through personal experience in the various particular jobs. A complete 'job analysis', as it is called, is so important in vocational selection, that any psychologist undertaking it must be prepared to spend some time learning and doing the various jobs involved. This may appear a counsel of perfection, on most occasions quite impracticable, because of the time involved. It indicates, however, the ideal which must be as closely approached as possible.

In the light of the 'job analysis' steps must be taken to devise methods of determining those among the applicants whose qualifications conform most closely to the requirements of the job. These methods will be, for the most part, test methods, but, in view of the fact already noted, that no reliable methods of testing character and personality are yet available, other methods of assessing personality traits, such as the interview, grading methods, and rating scales, must be included in the procedure.

As regards the testing, either of two procedures may be followed, either of two types of test being adopted. These two types are generally spoken of as the 'synthetic' and 'analytic' types respectively. The synthetic type of test involves presenting the testee with a test situation, which, as nearly as possible, calls for the same responses and actions as are called for in the real situation. The analytic type, on the other hand, consists of a series of separate tests, each of which is intended to test a mental or motor function, which plays an essential part in the work itself.

The synthetic type of test was first employed by Münsterberg.[1] The object was to test an individual's fitness for the position of electric car driver. Two points interested the car company on whose behalf Münsterberg was working. On the one hand they required drivers who would drive at

[1] *Psychology and Industrial Efficiency*, Chapter X.

a reasonably rapid rate. On the other hand they required drivers who would avoid accidents. The two qualities may obviously be in some respects inconsistent with one another, but the limits of efficiency on both sides are fixed by the conditions of practical life. By slow and careful driving it may be possible to avoid accidents altogether, but a certain speed must be maintained, and the driver who is too slow must therefore be regarded as inefficient, independently of the fewness of accidents. In the same way, a man may be a very fast driver, but have so many accidents as to be altogether too expensive for the company.

In order to solve the problem of measuring beforehand in the laboratory the probable efficiency as a car driver of any individual, Münsterberg devised a very ingenious test presenting very much the same kind of situation with which the car driver is actually faced in practical life. He took a card and divided it into squares, 26 lengthwise, and 9 cross-wise. At either side of the central row of squares he drew heavy lines to indicate the car lines. The four rows of squares on either side were occupied irregularly with the numbers 1, 2, and 3, in red or in black, no square having more than one number occupying it. The numbers had definite significations. Number 1 meant a pedestrian, number 2 a horse, number 3 a motor. The pedestrian was supposed to be able to move one square, the horse two squares, the motor three squares, while the car was coming up and passing. The black colour indicated traffic moving parallel to the car lines, and these numbers therefore only concerned the car driver as distracting elements. The red colour indicated traffic moving so as to cross the car lines. A red 1 therefore on the row next the lines, a red 2 in the second row, a red 3 in the third row from the lines, would be on the lines when the car came to that point, and the corresponding square therefore represented a danger point. Each square on the car line was lettered from A to Z, as the case might be.

Twelve such cards, each provided with a handle by which it could be removed by the experimenter, so as to expose the next, were laid one upon another under a sheet of glass, against which they were pressed by a spring underneath. Over the glass passed a belt of black velvet, with suitable openings at intervals, so as to enable the subject to see the whole breadth of the cards for five rows of squares. This belt was moved by a handle which was turned by the subject at his own rate. He started with the first card, and moving the belt while he observed through the opening, he called out the danger points, the letters being recorded by the experimenter. When the card was completed the experimenter withdrew it, exposing the next, and at the same time the next window came into position to enable the subject to begin at the beginning once more, and observe the new card in the same way as the previous one. The whole series of twelve was worked through in this way, the total time for the series being recorded.

The results of the experiment were expressed in three numbers, the first representing the time taken, the second the danger points omitted, the third the letters wrongly called, that is when there was no danger. Münsterberg neglected the last—wrongly it appears to the writer since, under the conditions of practical life, these represented unnecessary slowing of the rate of movement that would not be represented in the time under experimental conditions —and he expressed the efficiency of each individual by adding the time taken to ten times the number of omissions, thus reckoning one omission as equal to ten seconds extra time. Absolute inefficiency in regard to the occupation of car driver would then be represented by a number exceeding a limit determined in relation to the normal or best performance, and this limit might be exceeded either by too long time being taken, or by too many omissions being made, or by a combination of these defects. Actually Münsterberg took certain arbitrary limits of efficiency, both as regards time, and as regards number of omissions, but there is obviously no need for this arbitrariness, since the conditions of the experiment itself can be made to supply the limits.

Münsterberg's principles have since been applied, with certain modifications, to the testing of electric car drivers in

Hamburg. A report by Muscio, published by the Industrial Fatigue Research Board as Report No. 12, describes the method of testing as follows:

'The subject stands before an endless black band about 13 cm. broad, a length of about 130 cm. being visible, which travels towards him at a constant rate. Single holes and pairs of holes appear in this band at various distances from one another, the former indicating pedestrians and the latter vehicles. By means of a series of lamps, any single hole or pair of holes can be illuminated at different distances from the subject. The danger from a "vehicle" is always greater than that from a "pedestrian", and the danger from either is increased in proportion to its nearness to the subject. According to the degree of danger, one of three responses is required: the ringing of a bell with the foot, the moving of a lever with the left hand, and the "putting on a brake" with the right hand. The conditions in which these responses are respectively required are defined.

'On either side of the moving band, and at some distance from it, are two boxes, either of which can be illuminated independently of the other. These, when illuminated, represent sudden emergences of pedestrians or vehicles from either side of the track, and the reactions then required are the same as those required for corresponding stimuli on the moving band. Finally, a coloured light, situated some distance from the apparatus, is switched on and off intermittently, and the subject is required to count the number of times this occurs. All stimuli and reactions are recorded on an electrically driven smoked drum.'

Paris Transport have elaborated these methods of testing drivers of vehicles, and have supplemented them with analytic tests of various kinds. In the test developed from that of Münsterberg, the testee is seated in the driver's seat of a stationary motor bus in a darkened room. On the wall facing the driver is projected a busy street scene. The picture fills the wall, and when the motor engine is started the illusion of a bus travelling through a busy street is perfect. Various incidents occur, as, for example, a cyclist falling in front of the bus, as he comes out of a cross street, the whole being most realistic, the driver meanwhile reacting to the various emergencies, and his reactions being recorded. The same general principles were also adopted by Viteles, in a test for motor-car drivers, and by the present writer in a test for tank drivers, which, with the rapid development of tank warfare became obsolete almost while it was in process of being constructed. This last case admirably illustrates the limitations and defects of the synthetic type of test. There are only certain kinds of occupational situation, such as the driver situation, which can be usefully dealt with by the synthetic type, and any radical changes in that situation inevitably affect the usefulness of the test.

The analytic method of testing is normally based on a preliminary job analysis, which may, however, vary through a wide range in the degree of detail in which it is carried out. The procedure consists essentially in testing separately, by means of a battery of individual tests, the particular processes or functions involved in the work to be performed. In many cases the different types of test to be employed are already available, as a result of the development of the psychological study of individual differences, and the only thing to be done is to adapt appropriate kinds of material for the particular kinds of work to particular types of test. When new types of test have to be employed, the procedure already described must of course be followed.

A simple illustration may be taken from Münsterberg's[1] early work. He had to test candidates for the telephone service. He decided that the functions and characteristics requiring to be tested were 'memory, attention, intelligence, exactitude, and rapidity'. Tests of all these were already available. The tests he employed were the memory span (digits) test, the cancellation test, an association (mixed

[1] *Psychology and Industrial Efficiency*, Chapter VIII.

relations or analogies) test, the bisection of lines test, a rapidity of movement test, an aiming test, and a free association test. In order to grade the subjects on the results of all the tests, Münsterberg graded them for each test separately, and then took the average grading in all the tests as the final grade. This procedure is of course open to the serious objection that it involves giving equal weight to all the tests, when the different elementary processes tested may be, and most probably are, of different importance in the complex result, but it has at least the merit of convenience and simplicity, and it is a comparatively easy matter to weight any test or test to any desired amount. On the other hand it means the substitution of practical rule of thumb for exact mathematical methods, and so far cannot *prima facie* claim the same scientific validity as the results obtained by employing the correlation coefficient. Münsterberg's subjects were all employees of a telephone company, and their grading in the tests as thus obtained was compared with their grading for efficiency by the telephone company after three months' service. Unknown to the investigator, the company when selecting the subjects to be tested had included some of their most efficient operators. The result was a complete vindication of the psychological tests. The tests placed these subjects at the top. Further, those who were at the bottom of the list in the tests had already in the three months been found inefficient by the company. Of course there were some discrepancies between the test order and the practical efficiency order because of the sources of error by which either of the gradings might be affected. The experiment, however, showed conclusively that a few minutes' testing with appropriate tests could determine the probable efficiency of a telephone operator with an accuracy at least equal to that of a determination based on three months' trial.

For a number of years all candidates for apprenticeship in the printing trade in Edinburgh have been tested at the George Combe Psychological Laboratory there. A general analysis was first made of the kinds of work involved in a large printing works, undertaking practically all types of printing, and of the main psychological and motor processes entering into each kind of work. A scheme of testing was then decided on, which with a few modifications of detail has been found to work satisfactorily. In addition to a medical examination, and educational tests in English and arithmetic, all the candidates are given two group tests of intelligence, a verbal and a non-verbal, and tested individually for discrimination and choice time, ability to divide attention, rapidity, precision, and control of hand movement, aesthetic judgment, and colour vision.

Under certain circumstances a job analysis, in any real sense, may be impracticable. An alternative procedure must then be adopted. A number of recognized types of psychological tests, presumably tests of abilities involved in the work, may be selected. This battery of tests may be given to a group of workers, whose efficiency is already known, and who have been graded for efficiency by foreman or manager. The selected group should approximate normal distribution in their efficiency grading, or at least contain a certain number of superior, an equal number of inferior, and about twice that number of average workers. With such a group a measure of validation can be obtained by comparing the scores in the battery as a whole, as well as the scores for the individual tests, with the known efficiency of the subjects, as assessed by foreman or manager. This comparison can be made most satisfactorily, from a theoretical point of view, by the calculation of correlation coefficients. If the correlation of the battery scores with the efficiency assessments is reasonably high, we argue that the battery as a whole is reasonably valid. As regards the individual tests, those which show a high correlation may be retained, and those which show a low correlation discarded, and we are left with a fairly satisfactory series of tests for practical use as a selection battery.

Described in this way, the method, which may be called the 'empirical' method, appears very simple. In practice it is neither very simple, nor, as a rule, very satisfactory. The determination of the extent, to which there is a reasonable degree of correlation, involves the employment of somewhat elaborate methods of calculating correlation coefficients. The value of a correlation coefficient varies between $+1$ for complete agreement, and -1 for complete inverse relationship, but unless the coefficient is very high or very low—in the region of $+\cdot8$ or $+\cdot9$, or the same values with a negative sign—it is by no means easy to decide how much practical significance we can attach to it. Statisticians play gaily with correlation coefficients of the order of $\cdot3$ and $\cdot4$, and mathematically these may be just as interesting as coefficients of the order of $\cdot9$, but the overmastering practical interest is whether a test is testing what we want it to test. Hence a coefficient of $\cdot3$ or $\cdot4$ is rather poor pabulum for such practical interest, no matter what mathematical explanation and qualification it may carry with it. This may appear unjust to the statistician, but it is inevitably the view the practical man takes. For the practical man the only satisfying evidence of the value of a test is its proved validity in the cold light of subsequent experience. This is the acid test of all selection methods.

CHARACTER AND PERSONALITY

It has already been pointed out that, while the psychologist has been able to devise suitable and adequate tests for capacities and aptitudes, representing what, without the danger of serious misunderstanding, might be called the intellectual side of the human being, there is another side of human nature at least equally important in industry, as in social life, namely the emotional and volitional side—temperament, character, personality—where the psychologist has not had the same success. Not that the psychologist has been remiss in his attempts to devise test methods appropriate to this field, and has not attained a measure of success, as far as laboratory methods with laboratory apparatus are concerned. But the simple fact is that, up to the present time, no method of testing in this field has been made available for general employment, in the way we can employ tests of the Binet type, or of the American Army type, no test method which can be expected to give a reasonably definite quantitative assessment, in terms of intelligible, and generally acceptable, units, nothing in fact even remotely resembling a measuring rod.

This does not mean that no practically useful method of assessing emotional, temperamental, and personality characteristics is available. It is possible to refine and standardize methods of judging at least, if not assessing quantitatively, such characteristics of an individual, methods which have been widely employed from very early times, and which are employed every day by employers in engaging employees, but which, without refining and standardization, are very unreliable. The reference is to the method of the interview. The interview is a necessary accompaniment of test methods in any case, but unless it is used rightly, it may give very misleading results. On the analogy of job analysis, it is essential that the interviewer should have a clear idea of the qualities he is seeking to note and assess. The general plan of the interview should therefore be drafted beforehand. From the nature of the case, it is not possible to make the interview stereotyped, if it is to be enlightening. Moreover, as in the case of individual testing, with a scale of the Binet type, which itself partakes somewhat of the nature of an interview, it is of the first importance that *rapport* should be established between interviewer and interviewed at the very outset, before the interview proper begins. The personal relations between interviewer and interviewed may make all the difference between a good interview and a bad—good or bad from the point of view of both.

It is important that the interviewer record his impressions in as definite a form as possible. Either of two methods is available. He may use a 'grading method' or a 'graphic rating method'. For the grading method, he should, in his preliminary draft, tabulate the various qualities, which he wishes to observe, and, distinguishing, say, five different grades, assign the individual subject a grade A, B, C, D, or E, or a grade 1, 2, 3, 4, or 5, for each of these qualities. Alternatively, using a graphic method, he may take a line, horizontal or vertical, for each of the qualities, divide it into divisions according to the number of degrees in the possession of each quality he can express definitely in words, write these words under, or opposite, the respective divisions of his line, and indicate the point at which he would place each individual interviewed, for each of the qualities, by a mark on the appropriate line. This second method certainly gives a more refined method of marking. Whether the total effect is a more accurate representation of the personality as a whole, it is difficult to say. With a trained interviewer—for the interviewer requires training—either method will certainly give a more accurate, and very much more reliable result, than will dependence on any kind of intuitive judgments, or 'hunches'.

CHAPTER V

SCIENTIFIC MENTAL ENGINEERING

IT can scarcely be too often reiterated that we are merely at the beginning of an applied psychology of industry, as far as vocational testing is concerned. There is grave danger lest the undoubtedly great success which has attended the efforts of scientific-management engineers and those of British and American Army psychologists, and the equally great ignorance on the part of the industrial community regarding things psychological, should lead to an uncritical attitude towards mental tests and their present possibilities, which can only spell disaster in the long run. Much has been achieved, but much is still to do, before the genuinely scientific psychologist can be satisfied with the situation. A few years ago the psychologist could not get the industrial world to listen to him at all; when he spoke of the possible applications of mental tests in industry or in business, he was met on all hands with an incredulous smile and a shrug of the shoulders. All that has changed. The demand from the same quarter for psychological service has become insistent, and tends to be somewhat embarrassing. The uncritical attitude has swung round to the other extreme. It is well, therefore, that the exact position should be made perfectly clear, and that the requirements of this branch of applied psychology, in order to secure assured, steady, and continuous progress in the future, should be definitely known.

The first essential is that there should be close co-operation, not only among psychologists, but between psychologists and representatives of the practical interests involved, the interests both of the management and of the worker. As regards co-operation among psychologists, that scarcely requires argument. The task is not a task for one psychologist, or two or three psychologists, but for the whole psychologist strength of a nation. One of the results of the present movement will most certainly be the establishing of a new profession, the profession of 'psychologist'; and the establishing of a new profession on a broad and firm basis is no mean task. Moreover, the development of 'mental engineering' is a national service of the first order of importance. An American Army psychologist of the First World War, speaking of reconstruction after that war, says: 'Whether the reconstruction is military or non-military, the need of co-operative studies of vital mental problems and of co-operative efforts at scientific mental engineering will certainly not be less important for society than the scientific and engineering problems that concern material things.'

But the co-operation of the practical man is no less essential. The psychologist working alone cannot wholly determine either the practical problems involved, or the practical adequacy of the solutions he proposes. While the psychologist can perhaps lay down the general lines of industrial psychology, the numerous special problems presented by each particular industry can only be clearly defined by those who have actual working experience of the industry. The same principle holds of all branches of applied psychology. The general lines of the science may be laid down by the psychologist; the numerous special problems must be determined by those who have practical experience of the branch of activity which is studied, be it education, medicine, or business. There must be co-operation, therefore, between psychologist and practical man. Neither can do without the other, and neither can take the place of the other. Perhaps the psychologist has in the past been less likely to forget this than the practical man. For it does not take the psychologist long to discover in actual experimental work, that processes and factors he had considered most important on *a priori* grounds may be relatively insignificant in the ultimate outcome compared with factors which in his ignorance of the details of the complex process he had entirely overlooked. On the other hand, the practical man, with his practical experience of the work and its outcome, has in the past been much more apt to despise the elaborate technique of the experimental psychologist. He has readily acknowledged the importance of the expert knowledge and skill of the trained chemist or electrician, but it has until very recently been a much more difficult matter to get him to defer in the same way to the trained experimental psychologist. Psychology had first to make good its footing. It is by no means certain that this phase of the situation is wholly past yet, but it is rapidly passing.

In the sphere of vocational testing the special work for which there is most pressing need at the present time is the attainment of definite knowledge regarding the various physical and mental requirements of various industrial and economic tasks. The psychologist's own special task is necessarily held up until such knowledge is available. This is precisely the kind of work in which the co-operation of the practical man is most essential. The experience of the past few years has shown that it is a comparatively simple matter to secure the co-operation of employers and managers. Accumulating evidence can easily be brought forward to show the great increase in output and diminution in expenses that have followed upon systematic vocational testing and placement in individual instances where tests have been applied. But there has hitherto been a tendency on the part of the worker to regard the intervention of the psychologist with suspicion. No satisfactory progress is possible until this suspicion is removed. The co-operation of the workers themselves is no less important than the co-operation of the management. It ought to be made quite clear that the psychologist is not working in the interest of the employer, but in the interest of the industry at large, of the community, and of humanity. As a psychologist he is concerned solely with an impartial study of the facts. Knowledge of the facts is as much in the interest of the worker as of the employer. 'Facts are chiels that winna ding' is a popular saw in Scotland, that might be taken as a motto by all science, and not least by industrial psychology. Knowledge of the facts of vocational fitness and unfitness cannot be regarded as the privilege and the interest of any particular class in the

4

community. Not only is the success of any industry in the long run the concern of the worker as much as of the employer, but success or failure in one's life vocation touches the worker even more intimately, and industrial prosperity as well as individual happiness and content is the concern of every member of the community.

In order to make this co-operation effective it is desirable that a central institute of industrial psychology with regional institutes, associated preferably with universities, should be established, and that the council of these institutes should adequately represent the different interests involved, not merely the interest of the psychologist but that of the practical man as well, and not merely the interest of the employer but that of the employee also.[1] The function of such institutes should be in the first instance to co-ordinate research bearing on all the human problems demanding solution in industrial life. But they must not only co-ordinate research; they must also initiate research. In order to perform adequately this, the most responsible of their functions, the institutes must rely on the real, and not merely the nominal, co-operation of employer and worker alike. Practically this would probably mean that the central and regional institutes should be in direct touch both with employers' federations and with trade unions, or at least with corresponding bodies, and these bodies in turn would direct part of their activities towards work along the lines of industrial psychology. A further function of the central institute would be to exercise some kind of supervision over the training and qualifications of those psychologists who undertook industrial work.

This central institute would thus act as the heart and brain of a complex organization directed towards the practical application in industry and commerce of the results of all research and of all knowledge bearing upon the welfare and efficiency of the human factor in industry. What might be

[1] The National Institute of Industrial Psychology in this country is such a body, and ought to represent, and receive the support of, the interests involved, the psychologist, the employer, and labour.

described as fragments of the skeleton of such an organization may be said to be already in existence in the appointments committees of various universities—Oxford, Cambridge, Edinburgh, etc.—and in employment and labour bureaux of various kinds. Two clearly defined functions of such bodies are indicated, both representing the necessary complement to the research work stimulated by the central and regional institutes, and perhaps carried out either by psychologists working directly under their control in laboratories or in factories and the like, or by research workers in the psychology departments of the various universities.

The first of these functions is to institute and co-ordinate actual testing work. The practical arrangements for this might differ according to differing local circumstances. In the case of the appointments committees of universities, and of all similar institutions, these ought to have at their disposal information not only regarding the educational careers of all those who are registered in their books, but also regarding their physical and mental efficiency, general and special, as determined by some recognized system of tests. It is perhaps not too much to claim that the intelligence testing, already prescribed by some American universities as part of the preliminary examination before admission of a student to a course, is justified on grounds both of social and of educational policy. This arrangement would provide for the testing of all students entering universities or technical colleges. Similar arrangements ought to be made in connexion with all educational institutions, and particularly the public primary, secondary, and continuation schools. The actual practical work of testing university students would naturally be undertaken by the physiology and psychology departments. The best provision for such work in connexion with the schools would probably be secured by the establishment of central psychological clinics by the various education authorities, under the superintendence of specially appointed school psychologists, and the making of the mental testing and grading of all children part of the responsibility of such psychologists.

The second function of the appointments committees and employment bureaux would be to act as information agencies, on the one hand, by keeping a record of the physical and mental requirements of economic tasks, as these were determined, and of the physical and mental grading, both general and special, together with the educational and other qualifications of all individuals registered in their books; and, on the other hand, receiving in the usual way, and keeping a record of, the notifications of vacancies in the different industries, as well as a record of the steps taken to fill these vacancies, and of the after-careers of all their nominees who have in this way been placed in the various industries.

It will be noted that these proposals contain no more than the necessary provision for the adequate performance of the functions for which such bodies as appointments committees and employment bureaux were originally called into existence. It is no secret that these have in the past been a great disappointment to their sponsors. The reason is not far to seek. The means to hand were utterly inadequate for the attainment of the end desired. Essential information was not available, and essential machinery was non-existent. This is a matter in which we cannot live from hand to mouth as we have been trying to do in the past, and we cannot hope to improvise successfully except at enormous cost in money and in human material. During the two World Wars the British improvisations were wonderful, but they were terribly expensive. The more complex the need the more difficult the improvisation of the means to satisfy it, and the more expensive—out of all proportion. The problems of peace are infinitely more complex than the problems of war.

To return to our main topic. For vocational testing the immediate needs, as the industrial psychologist sees them, are: (1) adequate specification of the physical and mental requirements of various economic tasks; (2) tests sufficiently comprehensive, and sufficiently delicate and accurate, to give us reliable information regarding the corresponding capacities of human beings. These are the two points towards which research must at present, and for some time to come, be

directed. In the meantime, however, the industrial psychologist possesses satisfactory tests by means of which he can
grade general intelligence. He also possesses the means of
testing special capacities where a demand for such testing
has arisen. He is prepared to go on with the application of
those tests he has to industrial life, confident that he is able
to perform valuable service, even as things are.

But the psychologist least of all is likely to forget that there
are characteristics of human nature, and there are physical
and social conditions, upon which the efficiency and success
of an individual may depend, which are not touched by his
tests except in the most indirect fashion, if at all. Hence he
must not lend himself to the misleading of the public by
professing to do more than he can do. Individual efficiency
and success in industry may depend upon permanent
psychological factors, such as temperament, or taste, or
disposition, or character. Or it may depend upon temporary
psychological conditions of an emotional nature, such as
those which determine social unrest. So far, then, his general
and vocational tests are not available. It by no means follows
that his expert knowledge and advice may not be industrially
useful in such cases. Even where the factors affecting
industrial efficiency and success are physical, the work of the
industrial psychologist may still be valuable in tracing out
the physiological and psychological results of physical
conditions. After all, vocational testing is but one branch
of his work.

CHAPTER VI

EFFICIENCY OF WORK

THE field of vocational testing is almost the latest economic field which the modern applied psychology has entered, and the results so far secured in this field, however important they may ultimately turn out to be, are neither so numerous nor so striking as the results achieved in some other fields. The first direction in which what has become modern industrial psychology made a substantial stride forward was the study of the conditions determining efficiency of work. Perhaps this is still the direction in which the greatest progress has been made. It is certainly the direction in which the most striking industrial results have been forthcoming.

The conditions determining efficiency of work represent a wide field for psychological study. Naturally, therefore, we must not suppose that the task of the psychologist has been carried anywhere near completion in this field, or that there are now few problems awaiting solution. This is indeed very far from being the case. Nevertheless in this field the applied psychologist can point to many important investigations which have been carried out, and to many economically valuable conclusions which have been established, and he can fairly claim that in this field at least his science has justified its existence, in actual achievement as well as in promise for the future.

The study by the physiologist and the psychologist of the work curve—that is the curve representing variations in the efficiency of work from moment to moment during a continuous period—began in the physiological and psychological laboratories many years ago. It was motived in the main by medical and educational interests. The great object in the first instance was to study the effects of fatigue, and from the practical point of view to devise reliable tests for indicating the presence of fatigue. But these somewhat narrow aims were almost immediately overlaid, as the course of investigation led inevitably to a study of the various conditions, over and above fatigue, by which the efficiency of work may be affected. Investigators very soon realized the great complexity of their apparently simple initial problems. It is rather interesting to note that, while the problem of finding reliable tests for fatigue can hardly be regarded as solved even now, many of the problems to which the early investigations led have been solved, and their solutions have an economic significance scarcely, if at all, inferior to the economic significance of the primary problem.

THE WORK CURVE

Both muscular and mental work have been very carefully studied under laboratory conditions by physiologists and by psychologists. The two kinds of work demand different methods of investigation. We must therefore consider them separately. We may begin by considering muscular work. The apparatus usually employed is the *ergograph*. Various types of ergograph are in use, but nearly all embody the same general principles. Muscular contractions are made at regular intervals against a known resistance, and the amount of work done is continuously recorded in some way. Mosso's and Kraepelin's ergographs are the most familiar types. In both these cases the work is done by the contraction or bending of the middle finger of one hand. Arm and hand are clamped so as to make all movement impossible, leaving only the middle finger free. On this is fitted a metal cap, attached in such a way as to lift a weight with every contraction of the finger and through a distance proportional to the amount of the bending. The contractions of the finger are timed by the beats of a metronome. The total distance through which the weight is lifted in the course of the series of contractions constituting an experiment can be directly read from a scale or measured by the position at which the weight is left. There is also provision for yielding a record of each lift by means of an attached lever which marks on a regularly moving surface covered with smoked paper, thus yielding the work curve or *ergogram*.

Though the results obtained from ergograph work have in some respects been disappointing, nevertheless some interesting and important phenomena have been brought to light in the course of investigation. It has been shown, for example, that the maximum work is performed with a certain definite load, that whether we increase or diminish this load we get a decrease in the amount of work performed in a given time, provided that time be not too short. Further, it has been shown that the best work is done when a certain definite length of pause in the work is interposed at regular intervals. Both the most suitable load for any individual, and the most favourable arrangement of periods of work and rest for that load can be determined. Some figures cited by Myers in this connexion are very significant.[1] If the finger makes 30 contractions in 60 seconds with a certain load, two hours' rest is necessary for complete recovery. If, on the other hand, the finger makes 15 contractions in 30 seconds with the same load, only half an hour's rest is necessary. Hence in a two-hour period of work the second arrangement would give double the output. Some students working in the Combe Psychological Laboratory at Edinburgh obtained similar results. They compared different distributions of 60 contractions and a total pause period of 60 minutes, and found that by far the best work was done with the greatest distribution with which they worked, viz. 10 contractions and 5 rest pauses of 12 minutes each.

Again it has been shown in ergograph experiments that the fatigue produced—if it can be called fatigue—is simply fatigue for the particular circumstances. When the finger has been fatigued with a particular load to the point at which it ceases to contract altogether, the removal of part of the load has the effect of allowing the finger to resume its contractions almost, if not quite, to the original extent, and a new ergogram can be obtained for the reduced load.

Finally, some rather interesting experiments and results

[1] *Present-day Applications of Psychology.*

are described by Ash.[1] If, while a trace is being taken of the contractions of the middle finger, a lever is attached to the third finger and also one to the forefinger, and both these fingers are also attached to springs which will compel them if moved to overcome approximately the same resistance as the middle finger has to overcome, then, before the extent of the contractions of the middle finger shows any appreciable diminution, these other fingers will begin to be flexed, and the extent of these subsidiary contractions will progressively increase as the contractions of the middle finger diminish in extent, and as more and more effort is required to continue the work. On the other hand, if these fingers are kept immovable until the middle finger can no longer contract, and then released, contraction of the middle finger is again obtained, often with its original amplitude, and a new ergogram can be traced. It is possible, in fact, to obtain three successive ergograms from the middle finger by releasing the other fingers one at a time.

The practical bearing of these results will be considered in its proper place. In the meantime we must take up the consideration of the laboratory investigation of mental work. Detailed studies of the work curve in mental work were first made by Kraepelin and his students. In their chief experiments they employed the continuous addition of single digits as the mental work to be done, and the efficiency of the work was measured by the number and accuracy of such additions performed in unit time. It has been found that nothing is gained by making the work difficult, when our object is to get a work curve. The usual procedure is for the subject to go on continuously with his addition, while the experimenter gives a signal at regular intervals, say of a minute, and the subject makes a mark to indicate the point he has reached at each signal. This enables the course of the curve to be plotted, seeing that we can determine the work done from minute to minute.

As a result of such experiments we obtain a curve

[1] Ash, 'Fatigue and Its Effects upon Control,' *Archives of Psychology*, No. 31.

presenting at a first glance a somewhat irregular appearance. The irregularities are due mainly to 'spurts'. These may have various causes. Usually a subject starts with a spurt and finishes with a spurt—unless he is kept ignorant that the end of the work is at hand. The other spurts, occurring at irregular intervals between the beginning and the end of the work, may be due to the wandering of the subject's attention, to the idea, perhaps, coming into his mind that he is not getting on so rapidly as he might, to the desire to make up the loss due to real or imaginary waste of time, and so on. When we discount the effects of such spurts, we come to see that the work curve shows certain regular features which constantly reappear. There is an initial spurt, then a falling-off followed by a continuous and rapid rise in the curve; then there may be a slow rise for a longer time, to be followed sooner or later by a fall, gradual at first, but increasing, with possibly a final spurt at the end. These regular features are due to the operation of general factors determining the efficiency of all work. These general factors are four: practice, fatigue, what we call 'warming-up' to the work, and adaptation or 'settlement', that is the adapting of oneself to the conditions of the work and becoming able to ignore distracting influences.

Naturally the practice effect will vary according as the subject is expert at the kind of work or not. Where there is little or no practice-gain the effect of fatigue will show itself earlier; where there is a significant practice-gain, it will obviously for some time mask the effect due to oncoming fatigue. The two factors act in opposite directions. With respect to the effects due to 'warming-up' and 'settlement' respectively, it is very difficult to separate them. Both show themselves at the beginning of the work, and co-operating with the practice-effect, cause the steep rise which the curve of work shows at that stage. The 'warming-up' effect shows itself the earlier of the two, and disappears the more rapidly on cessation of the work, but it is not at all certain that the difference is such as to enable us to separate the effects of the two factors experimentally.

Consider now the effect of pauses. A pause will allow a measure of recovery from such fatigue as is present, and hence improve the efficiency of the work. On the other hand it will also allow the human machine to grow cold, and, if it is prolonged, will cause the gain due to 'settlement' to disappear, and lastly perhaps even the gain due to practice. Hence a pause in the work may produce a somewhat complex effect, and may not result in a net gain as far as output is concerned. The net gain or loss will depend on the combined influence of the factors involved. We can by experiment find a pause of such length that the efficiency of work before and after will be exactly equal. This is called the 'equilibrial pause'. A pause of such a length as to give the greatest gain in efficiency can also be experimentally found. This is called the 'most favourable pause'.

The method by which these different pauses are determined is relatively simple. After, say, half an hour's work, different lengths of pause are tried. The result will give us the information we desire—for the individual and for the period of work. When we have determined the most favourable pause for any individual, it is also possible for us to measure certain of his characteristics which have a bearing on his efficiency as a worker and more particularly, his 'fatiguability'. In order to measure 'fatiguability' we take, say, an hour's work. The subject works for half an hour, then the most favourable pause is interposed, and then he works for the second half-hour. Let us suppose that in the first half-hour he adds 2,000 digits, and in the second half-hour after the pause 2,200. We compare this result with the result obtained in an hour's work without a pause. If in this case he adds 2,020 digits in the first half-hour, we should expect, assuming that the practice-gain is regular, and that there is no loss due to fatigue, that in the second half-hour he would add 2,200/2,000 of 2,020 = 2,222. He actually does 2,082. The fatigue due to the first half-hour's work has therefore diminished his efficiency by the difference 2,222 − 2,082 = 140. We take this diminution as a measure of his fatiguability, and we get a coefficient of fatiguability for the individual by expressing this as a fraction of the work we should have expected him to perform in the second half-hour. That is to say, $140/2,222$ is the coefficient of fatiguability for the individual. This number expresses the ease or difficulty with which he is fatigued by the work, according as it is large or small.

The methods of the laboratory in the study of work can be transferred practically unchanged to the factory. But in the factory the subject's task is usually so much more complex, and the working conditions so much less uniform, that clear-cut results are difficult to obtain. In any case the investigation cannot be carried out by the amateur, but requires the services of the expert psychologist, and the employment of the technical methods of the psychological laboratory. This is a truth which must be brought home to all who are directly interested in such matters, whether on the side of the management or on the side of the worker. The problems are scientific problems demanding the employment of scientific methods in their investigation, and highly trained technical skill in the investigator. To undertake such investigations without the necessary technical training in psychological methods would be as futile as to undertake the investigation of a complex chemical process without technical training in the methods of the chemical laboratory.

MOTIVES AND INCENTIVES

It may be taken as a fundamental principle, however apt we are to forget it, that whatever work we do is done because there is some motive for doing it. No human activity is motiveless. Moreover, the motive is a specific motive for that exact form of activity which takes place. There may of course be a general motive for activity as distinct from inactivity—the mere irksomeness of doing nothing, if we can put it no higher—but in addition there is the motive for that precise way in which we are active, for doing that very thing we do. A second fundamental principle is that the intensity with which we are active will be in proportion to the strength of the motive which prompts the particular activity, up to the limit at which the motive becomes so overpoweringly strong as to impair the working power, or even inhibit it altogether, as when it takes the shape of violent emotion.

This is one of the most obvious points where the science of psychology carries on the analysis of the economist. The economist assumes the motive as motive in the abstract— for that is what it really amounts to—calling it perhaps self-interest. Ruskin's strictures on the science of economics because of this assumption are really, as we have already seen, wide of the mark. It is not the business of the economist to analyse and give an account of motives in the concrete, but it is the business of the psychologist. Whether the economist calls the motive 'self-interest' or an indeterminate 'X' is a matter of indifference as far as economic science is concerned. Plainly, however, it is not a matter of indifference as far as the understanding of the forces and elements in economic life is concerned. Hence it cannot be too frequently or too strongly emphasized that for the understanding of economic life in the concrete psychology is as important and as essential as economics. At the same time it must be remembered that even the psychologist is not entitled to pronounce regarding the use that may or ought to be made of any particular motive or incentive. All that the psychologist is called upon to do is to analyse the motives which actually operate, to determine the conditions under which they operate most powerfully, and to trace the psychological effects which follow their operation in the particular cases. The economist must go on to trace these effects in the economic sphere, and it is for the political and social philosopher to pronounce concerning their desirability or the reverse. Again it is necessary to emphasize the point. Psychology must not be made in any way responsible for some of that 'speeding-up' and over-driving in industry, which various scientific-management engineers have falsely attributed to psychology. All that psychology can be made responsible for is the devising of means for the attainment of an end which had been settled on independently of

psychology, and before recourse was had to the studies of
the psychologist. The psychological effects of 'speeding-up'
these scientific-management enthusiasts prudently ignore,
but these are as interesting and as significant to the
psychologist as the psychological methods by which it is
produced, and the economic, social, or political philosopher
neglects the findings of the psychologist in this regard at
his peril.

Since the beginning of the present century the attention
of the psychologist has been more and more concentrated on
the emotional, as distinct from the intellectual aspect of
human nature. On the practical side this becomes in the
main a study of motivation, the importance of which in all
fields of human behaviour and endeavour, including the
economic, only needs to be mentioned in order to be realized.
Psychological investigation in this branch of the science was
greatly stimulated by the work of McDougall, on the one
hand, and the work of the various representatives of the
analytic schools, Freud, Jung, and Adler, on the other.
Whatever our opinions with respect to the theories and
hypotheses, developed, formulated, and expounded by these
psychologists, we must admit the profound significance of
those deeper forces discussed by them on the relations
between employees and the management, and between
employees and one another, and the great influence exerted
by these relations on the efficiency of an industrial, or commercial undertaking, and, more generally, on the avoidance or
creation of industrial unrest and conflict. Unfortunately the
field is a highly controversial one, but the controversies are
rather battles about words and theories than about facts, and
these facts can be examined and organized, without com-
mitting ourselves to any ultimate theories.

Both McDougall and the psychoanalysts are apt to use
language which suggests that the human being, in what we
may call his deeper strata, is an assemblage of separate
agencies—McDougall's 'instincts', Freud's 'wishes', and the
like—which produce or cause certain forms of behaviour.
This suggests something like a revival of the old 'faculty'

psychology, more or less in the form in which we find it represented among the phrenologists. To some extent a tendency in this direction is due to, and inherent in, the nature of language itself, which, as the instrument of the intellect of man, meets formidable difficulties in seeking to express, without a great deal of circumlocution, what is deeper than the intellect, and, in its processes, radically different from the intellect. The tendency is one against which we must always be on our guard, in discussing the phenomena of motivation, and, perhaps more especially, when the motives under discussion are those of which the individual himself is largely unaware, at least in their naked form. In the discussion of motivation it is necessary to separate out, distinguish, and designate by definite names, the various motives or motive 'forces', but this does not make them entities and active agents. The only active agent is the human being as he exists at the moment he is acting. At that moment he may be actuated, or it might be better to say influenced, by a complex of motives, very difficult to analyse, even for himself.

With the proviso that there is no fundamental and characteristic human impulse, which may not enter into the complex of motives determining an individual's behaviour, during his working hours, or during his spare time, in or out of the factory, we may nevertheless select some which appear to be of primary importance, and predominating influence. Some psychologists might speak of these as instincts or drives or needs—the name does not matter greatly from a practical point of view, and from such a point of view it is perhaps better to avoid giving them any names suggestive of any theory, but to make categorical statements of fact. It is a fact that all normal human beings desire to stand for something among their fellows, or at least in their own estimation, not to be a mere cipher, to secure some sort of recognition. It is a fact that all normal human beings seek to escape from situations which are disagreeable or painful, and, failing escape, may attack and seek to destroy the source of the disagreeableness. It is a fact that all normal human beings seek to obtain possession of that which they value, either for the pleasure they may derive from its possession, or for the other sources of satisfaction which may be secured through its possession. The interplay of these and kindred impulses and desires, at all levels of awareness, plays a very important part in all human action in the economic field, as in family life and social relations.

Let us consider briefly the more or less direct operation of such fundamental human desires, as far as industrial activity is concerned. With the desire to secure some sort of recognition from, to be respected by, to stand well with, his fellows, and as a result to stand well in his own estimation, an individual will aim at securing at least equal status, equal wages, equal reputation with his fellows in the social circle to which he belongs, and this may affect every one and every-thing connected with, or belonging to, him, which in any way exercises an influence on social esteem in that circle. The desire to avoid, evade, or escape from the disagreeable is so universally characteristic of all living creatures, that it is difficult, in the case of the adult human being, to restrict its simple and direct operation to any one particular type of disagreeableness. The 'law of selection', as between the agreeable and the disagreeable, is very wide in the range of its operation, even under the most primitive conditions. The civilized adult, however, has become, as it were, so sophisti-cated, with respect to the agreeable and the disagreeable, that it is virtually impossible to trace the limits of its operation, all the more since there may be involved unconscious, as well as conscious, influences. The actual behaviour eventuating is apt to be further complicated, in the human being, as in the animal, by aggression being substituated for escape under certain circumstances. The desire to acquire, possess, and control objects to which value is attached, as themselves sources of satisfaction, or as means to the securing of other sources of satisfaction, is almost equally wide in its range. Since, however, in a modern civilized community wealth, as represented in money, is the most general means of securing satisfaction, this desire in its most simple and most direct operation is usually a desire for the possession of an increased supply of wealth in the form of money.

The intricate interweaving of these desires with one another, and with all the other impulses and desires, natural and acquired, renders the industrial situation in its motivation aspect one of such complexity, that its adequate discussion would itself require an entire volume. It is to this complex situation that we must look for guidance regarding the motives and incentives, which underlie the individual's economic and industrial activity, and to a large extent his efficiency as an active unit in the economic life of the community. To this complex situation we must also look for the understanding of the psychological conditions productive of industrial unrest and industrial conflict. The intimate personal interests of the individual, his family, his friends, his union, his tools, his job, and much else, become constituents of his larger social and economic personality, and circumstances affecting any of these may evoke the same emotional responses as if they affected his narrower individual self. Moreover, unless we bear in mind the further fact that motives and incentives may be operating, of which the individual himself is partly or wholly unaware, and that the reasons he may give for an action are not infrequently superficial rationalizations on his part, rather than the true reasons, our understanding may be quite inadequate and even misleading.

With these facts in mind, can we be surprised at the relative failure of incentives involving wage increases, bonus systems, profit-sharing, and the like, to produce the effects intended and expected? The proved inadequacy of any kind of financial incentive has, in recent times, stimulated deeper inquiry into the motives operating in industrial life. The psychiatrist, as well as the psychologist, has come into the picture. Unfortunately the psychiatry of to-day is obsessed with the abnormal, and its subjective orientation, under the influence of Freudian and kindred psychological theories, makes it a rather dangerous guide without that objective evaluation of the facts in which the psychologist has been trained. The only safety would appear to be in a team consisting of both psychologist and psychiatrist, with a physiologist in the background.

After a detailed consideration of the investigations that have been carried out in this field of motives and incentives, Viteles[1] summarizes in these words: 'The findings suggest that the level and consistency of production are determined by a wide variety of variables, which require careful study and control for the attainment of maximum yield, satisfaction, and fitness on the part of the individual worker.' And he quotes Kornhauser, one of the investigators in this field: 'Whatever the difficulties and whatever the poverty of present knowledge, the problems are so central and inescapable, and so clearly problems of industrial psychology—if it chooses to be a social science as well as a managerial technique—that it appears well worth our while canvassing the possibilities of further promising research in the field. Among the few greatest questions of our age is that which asks what modern industry means to the individual worker with reference to his satisfactions and fullness of life.'

MENTAL SET OR ATTITUDE

The industrial activity of the human being may also be affected by psychological conditions, which can scarcely be classed under the head of motives, and for which a better designation is probably 'mental set' or 'attitude'. Some of these conditions may be of very much the same order as the motives prompting to the work itself. The emotional mood, for example, of the worker would represent one such condition, scarcely distinguishable from what we have just been considering. Other conditions which are not primarily of an emotional character may arise from the circumstances under which the work is done, or the worker's belief regarding the uninterestingness, irksomeness, hardness, or the reverse, of the work he is doing. Some of these conditions will come up for fuller consideration later. At present two important factors, both of which have been rather carefully

[1] *Industrial Psychology*, p. 585.

studied by the psychologist in other fields, seem to deserve more particular mention. These are *interference* and *suggestion*.

The phenomena of *interference* may show themselves in various ways, and affect the efficiency of work in different degrees, but the general principle is relatively easy to understand. If a muscular or mental act A is frequently followed by the act B, the performance of the act A will tend to produce at least a readiness in the human system for the act B, and any attempt to follow A with a different act C will be hampered or impeded by the connexion already established between A and B, and the fact that the muscular or mental system has got a setting for the performance of B after A. The 'set' is itself an advantage, for it facilitates the performance of the acts one after another in a regular succession. If B and C follow A indifferently, the advantage of this facilitation is lost; if B usually follows A, but now and then C is interpolated irregularly, there will be *interference* in addition to the loss of facilitation. If, for example, we go down a column of two-figure numbers adding and subtracting 8 alternately, we shall find that we take considerably longer time, and feel the task harder, than if we add 8 or subtract 8 every time. So in a piece of work, if the workman must continually change over from one process to another, or if he has to interrupt a regular succession of acts by every now and then performing a different act, the rate and efficiency of the work will be impaired, especially if, and in proportion as, the interruptions are irregular.

The factor of *suggestion* may operate in a still more striking way in affecting an individual's working efficiency. If the worker is induced to believe that his task is very difficult he reacts to it as a difficult task, and the amount of work performed may in consequence be greatly reduced, and the amount of fatigue developed correspondingly increased. The opposite effect will be produced if the suggestion that the work is easy can be successfully conveyed. Hollingworth and Poffenberger[1] quote from Jastrow a very interesting

[1] *Applied Psychology*, p. 130.

and illuminating illustration. For the tabulation of some census returns a new and elaborate method was introduced for indexing on the card-index system. The clerks were at the outset given the idea that the work was intricate and difficult, and that it demanded exceptional ability, application, and skill. After a preliminary training for about five weeks in the various operations involved, they were able on the average to complete 500 cards per day. But to do this seemed to demand such feverish effort on the part of the workers that they protested against the attempts which were being made to spur them on by the publication of records, and this had to be discontinued. Some 200 new clerks were taken on after the work had got well started. These were distributed among those already at work. The new clerks had none of the preliminary training of the original workers, nor had they the conviction that the work was specially hard and fatiguing. On the contrary, they saw every one around them working rapidly, and with apparent ease. The result was that in three days some of the newcomers had reached the 500 mark; in a week nearly all had done so. Before the work was over one of the new clerks actually succeeded in completing as many as 2,230 cards in one day—more than had originally been regarded by the clerks first employed as four days' hard work. Perhaps no more striking illustration could be given of the potency of the mental factor in our daily work.

There is something of irony in the fact that the same man, who at a football match on Saturday spends every ounce of his energy, that his side may win the game, and struggles on for that end when he is bruised, bleeding, covered with mud, and almost at his last gasp, may on Monday in the factory display quite a different spirit, may even on occasion show himself a slacker and a shirker. During the war the spirit in many factories was the spirit of the football field. Of course it is not wise economy to work with the same energy and abandon as we play football, nor is it possible. But it is the spirit of the worker, and of the whole body of workers, that matters, and it is there that the psychological problem lies.

What are the psychological causes determining the psychological phenomena in the two cases? How far, and under what conditions, is it possible to make the psychological causes which operate in the one case operate in the other as well, and if they do so operate, what further psychological effects arise, which must be taken into account in determining practical policy? These are questions which press for solution, but their solution is not even in sight.

CHAPTER VII

THE STUDY OF FATIGUE

FATIGUE has already been mentioned as one of the general factors determining efficiency of work. Its importance from that point of view has long been recognized. As already indicated it was the study of fatigue that led to the study of the varying efficiency of work and the other factors, additional to fatigue, which play a part in producing the variations. We must in the present chapter take up the consideration of fatigue in fuller detail, and see what light physiological and psychological investigation can throw on its nature and production.

What is fatigue? The answer may be given in subjective or in objective terms. Subjectively, fatigue is a state of consciousness, usually more or less disagreeable, determined by a mass of sensations, sometimes with fair definiteness localized, and vague feelings which are not localized. The state is one which everybody has experienced. It is accompanied by a disinclination for work and a desire to rest, with a felt incapacity for work added. Such a definition, however, is of very little service even to pure psychology, and of no use at all outside the limits of that science. The state as described is not clearly marked off from the state we call 'boredom', which is due mainly to lack of interest rather than the expenditure of energy in activity; and further, the feeling of incapacity for work may be more or less illusory, if we take the quantity and quality of the work done under these conditions as a criterion. 'Weariness' is probably a better word to employ for the subjective state, inclusive both of boredom and of real fatigue, and we should always remember that this subjective 'weariness' does not necessarily imply diminished capacity for work, nor does its absence imply that the capacity for work is not really diminished. If we define fatigue in objective terms, we are practically compelled to define it in terms of output. That is, we have to define it as a state of lowered efficiency in the organism, brought about by the expenditure of energy in doing work, and showing itself either in impairment of the quality of the work subsequently done, or in diminution of the quantity, or in both. This definition by no means escapes all the difficulties. Considerable fatigue may apparently be present without any of these objective results being produced. At a certain stage, as Myers points out,[1] fatigue may produce a general excitement with extravagance in the expenditure of energy, and as a result increased output with no falling-off in quality. Hence, as we shall see presently, arises the difficulty of finding reliable tests for fatigue.

Most of what we know with scientific accuracy regarding fatigue as a state of the organism we owe to the labours of the physiologist. The main facts which he has established are the following: When energy is expended in the doing of work by a muscle there is consumption of energy-producing material, and the production in the muscle itself of substances which are designated 'toxic' substances, that is, which act as poisons to the tissues. The substance in the muscles which produces the energy, which acts therefore as fuel, is glycogen, and the chief toxic substances produced are carbon dioxide and lactic acid. Glycogen in the form of 'animal starch' is stored in the liver and the muscle cells. The liver acts as a storehouse for the muscles, and in strenuous muscular work the blood brings glycogen from this storehouse to keep the muscle supplied. Complete fatigue would be produced if this store were exhausted. That does not happen, however, for the accumulation of toxic substances in the muscles produces effects tending to the cessation of muscular activity long before this stage of complete exhaustion of the energy-producing substance is reached.

The physiologist may be experimenting with a single muscle and the nerve attached—the 'nerve-muscle preparation'. If, in this case, he stimulates the muscle with electric shocks, and keeps on stimulating it, there is a gradual

[1] *Mind and Work*, p. 46.

diminution and ultimate cessation of muscular contractions, due partly to the using-up of glycogen and partly to the accumulation in the muscle of toxic substances. If, however, the stimulation of the muscle is through a nerve, the muscle itself never reaches this stage of fatigue. It is protected by the so-called *end-plate* of the nerve, that is the structure in which the nerve terminates in the muscle. This yields to fatigue first and ceases to carry the stimulus to the muscle fibres. It is easy to show that this is the case by stimulating through the nerve until the muscle ceases to contract, and then transferring the stimulus to the muscle itself directly, when it is thrown into contraction once more and can be gradually fatigued as before.

In the intact organism, as distinct from the 'nerve-muscle preparation', the end-plates are also protected against fatigue by other processes. On the one hand the accumulation of toxic substances in the muscle affects the sensory nerve-endings in the muscle, and a nervous impulse is carried back to the spinal cord along the sensory nerve which has the effect of inhibiting or preventing the outgoing stimulus along the motor nerve to the muscle, and hence of the cessation of muscular contractions. Even this stage may not be reached owing to processes at a 'fatigue point' in the nervous system itself. The structural units of which the nervous system is built up are known as *neurons*. Each neuron consists of a nerve cell with various processes. The nerve fibres are all processes of neurons. It is generally held that the neurons are not directly continuous with one another, although nervous impulses pass from one to the other, and the points at which they become contiguous and at which impulses may pass are known as *synapses*. Now the consumption of energy within the nervous system has the same result as in the muscle. There is a using-up of energy-producing substance and an accumulation of toxic products, and this has the effect of increasing the resistance at the synapses. If the resistance at a synapse, across which the nervous impulse must pass to cause the muscle to contract, is increased, then a time will come when, unless the strength of the impulse is increased, it will be unable to overcome the resistance, and consequently there will be a cessation of activity in the muscle.

These facts enable us to explain some of the ergographic phenomena to which we have already drawn attention. The nervous impulses producing the muscular contractions are voluntary, that is they come from the higher nervous centres. Increase of resistance at a synapse will necessarily involve an increase of stimulus, if the muscular contractions are to be maintained. This is forthcoming by an effort of will. But this increase of stimulus means the liberation of more energy in the centres, and it may therefore have the effect of overcoming other synapse resistances, which were previously sufficient to protect the muscular structures corresponding from stimulation, but which are no longer sufficient. Hence the effect of the stimulus may extend to adjacent structures, and extend progressively, as the resistance of the original synapse increases, and as the energy liberated to overcome it increases in proportion. Hence in experiments with the ergograph, if the forefinger and third finger are left free they will begin to show contraction before the contractions of the middle finger show any significant diminution, because more and more energy requires to be liberated in the centres to keep the middle finger contracting. In the same way the pedestrian at the end of a long day's tramp walks with his whole body. With all this there is increasing inability to control the exact direction the liberated energy has to take.

The waste products which cause the various kinds of fatigue are taken up by the blood. Hence, theoretically, there can be no such condition as purely local fatigue. All production of waste products at one point must affect to a greater or less degree the organism as a whole. There is a well-known experiment which demonstrates this. If blood be transferred from a fatigued animal to an animal which has not been fatigued, the symptoms of fatigue shows themselves in the animal to which blood is transferred. On the other hand, there is no doubt that the fatigue can be relatively local. In that case the symptoms of fatigue will disappear with a change of activity. Moreover, cessation of activity may be due simply to lack of the necessary incentive. In this case there may be no real fatigue, either local or general, as can easily be shown by introducing the influence of an incentive.

It is thus possible for us, on the basis of the work of the physiologist, to get a clear and consistent idea, up to a certain point at least, of the nature of fatigue as a state of the organism. There is nothing to be gained by making too much of the distinction between mental fatigue and muscular fatigue. By mental fatigue we must understand, it is true, fatigue which has its origin in expenditure of energy and the accumulation of toxic substances in the central nervous system, and by muscular fatigue, fatigue which is due to the expenditure of energy and the accumulation of toxic substances in the muscle or group of muscles which have been active. But we have already seen that in the intact animal or organism there is an expenditure of nervous energy and an accumulation of waste products in the nervous centres in muscular activity, and it is impossible for the nervous centres to be active in the case of mental activity without contraction and tension in various groups of body muscles. Besides, the blood stream inevitably tends to spread the effects of fatigue with the toxic substances it carries, as we have just seen. Mental fatigue can also be relatively local, in which case change of the kind of activity will cause the symptoms of fatigue to disappear. The analogy to muscular fatigue is complete. One of the most interesting symptoms of oncoming mental—as of oncoming muscular—fatigue is loss of control over the direction of the nervous impulse. In the case of mental fatigue this shows itself in a wandering of the attention and an inability to keep the mental activity to the desired channel.

The important part which fatigue plays, both from the point of view of the health and welfare of the worker and from the point of view of the efficiency of the work, is sufficient explanation of the attention it has attracted from physiologists and psychologists. We have already seen that the systematic experimental study of work began in the attempt to determine some constant accompaniment and symptom of fatigue, which might be used as a practical test for its presence. Now that we realize the complexity of the conditions upon which fatigue depends, it need occasion no surprise that this problem of finding a reliable test for fatigue has proved very difficult of solution.

It is, of course, central or general fatigue that we wish to find a test for. And not only do we wish to find a test which will indicate the presence of fatigue; we also wish to be able to measure its amount. With the 'nerve-muscle preparation', or in any case where we could to an equal extent control all the conditions, we might measure fatigue in terms of the consumption of the energy-producing substance and the accumulation of waste products. In the intact organism, and more particularly in the human being, this method cannot be applied. Hence we are thrown back upon the symptoms of fatigue. Practically the human being regulates his activity by his subjective feelings—the feeling of weariness, with inability to concentrate the attention, and possibly headache. The unreliability of these symptoms as a test has already been pointed out. The feeling of weariness is not unknown in our own experience on a Monday morning, or when we are faced with a specially hard task. We do not necessarily impugn an individual's good faith by declining to accept his statement that he is tired as reliable evidence of fatigue. When the work is not particularly interesting the lure of leisure or amusement will readily induce a feeling of weariness that is genuine enough.

But if we rule out subjective feelings as a criterion for fatigue, what can we put in their place? The tests for fatigue which have been tried out in the laboratory fall into two groups—direct tests and indirect tests. The direct tests attempt to measure general efficiency (mental) directly by the quantity and quality of the performance in some kind of mental work; the indirect tests attempt to measure general efficiency by some subsidiary change, as it were, which takes place as a result of bodily or mental exertion. The former have usually been considered the more reliable, but they are subject to the disadvantage that the individual tested can readily simulate the symptoms of fatigue, and the simulation may even be quite unintentional and unconscious.

The direct tests which have been most frequently used are: (1) Dictation. This seems to have been first employed by Sikorsky as far back as 1879. The experiment has been repeated mainly as a class test in schools by a number of investigators. Fatigue is estimated by the number of spelling errors. Friedrich, using the test to trace the rise of fatigue during a school session, got 40 errors before the work began, 70 after one hour, 120 after two hours, 190 after three hours. This simple enumeration of errors without taking account of the work done is obviously inadequate. The main objection to the test, however, is the difficulty of standardizing it. We cannot easily get dictations of the same difficulty. Even if we could, we cannot simply equate one spelling error to another. Not only are words different as regards difficulty, but different words have different degrees of difficulty for different individuals at different times, and different kinds of error are symptomatic in different ways. (2) Cancellation, or some analogous test like McDougall's 'dot-marking' test, where small circles have to be dotted as they pass at a uniform rate across a slit at varying points along the slit. This test has considerable value. Unfortunately, however, it is a test in which performance is very much affected by practice, by adaptation, and possibly also by muscular fatigue. In measuring efficiency we must take two factors into account, the amount of work done and its accuracy. The simplest way is to take the product of the two, but this is not entirely satisfactory. In any case it is probable that variability in the efficiency from moment to moment is a better indication of incipient fatigue than efficiency itself. (3) Calculation. This is the test which has been most frequently employed. Simple additions of digits, or simple multiplications, are the most suitable arithmetical processes. The test is a fairly good one, but, like the last, it requires much care in the elimination of practice effects, and other effects which mask or simulate fatigue, and presents the same difficulty in interpreting the results.

While these may be regarded as the chief types of direct test used in laboratory work, they are by no means the only tests that have been so used. Ebbinghaus's combination test, and various memorizing tests must also be mentioned. These are generally open to rather serious objections, and the difficulty of marking the first is sufficient to put it out of court in the meantime.

The indirect tests are nearly all very interesting. In their case it is assumed that central fatigue is accompanied by deterioration in some subsidiary function tested, or by some symptom which can be observed and measured. Quite a number of indirect tests have been employed. Perhaps the most famous historically is the 'aesthesiometric index'. In this test we measure the smallest distance between two points touching the skin that enables the subject to say that there are two points. Orginally the most extravagant claims were put forward on behalf of this test. At the present time it is generally held that, while the aesthesiometric index may indicate the presence of fatigue, it is not at all reliable, especially as a measure of fatigue, since it may be affected by a number of other conditions. A similar test is the test of sensitivity to pain as measured by the instrument known as the 'algesimeter'. This too, is unsatisfactory. In fact it is not at all certain whether fatigue increases or diminishes sensitivity to pain. Tests of muscular efficiency have also been employed under the idea that central fatigue diminishes muscular efficiency. The chief difficulty with such tests, which seem fairly reliable though by no means delicate, is that they tend to develop local muscular fatigue with considerable rapidity so as to mask the effects of central fatigue. Reaction time and rate or rhythm of tapping have also been employed.

There is one objection to practically all these tests. As 'performance' tests they can be very easily manipulated by the subject, consciously or unconsciously, so as to simulate fatigue. The same objection is valid against a very interesting test recently used by Ash and also by the present writer.[1] That is the 'reversible perspective' test. It is well known that outline drawings of solids, which do not show perspective of any kind, are capable of being perceived in two ways, the mind as it were imposing upon them two different constructions. The 'stair' figure and Scripture's 'blocks' are two familiar examples of such figures. These figures are, however, too complex for use as a fatigue test. For this purpose a cube or a square pyramid should be chosen. Either can be seen in two ways, that is, with one or other or two sides towards the observer. It is impossible for an observer who has seen the two aspects to maintain either for any considerable length of time. In a few seconds the figure invariably 'reverses'. But although the observer cannot prevent 'reversal', he can control the rate of reversal, when he tries to produce it. This is the basis of the test. According to the underlying theory fatigue impairs control, and the result of impaired control is an inability to keep up our normal rate of voluntary reversal of these figures. The test seems to be a very delicate one, much more so than any of the others we have described, but unfortunately we have no means of objective control by which to check the rate of reversal.

Other indirect tests have been suggested and used, against which this objection is not valid, since they are tests of processes of which the subject is largely or wholly unconscious. Changes in respiration, or in the circulation of the blood as measured by pulse, blood-pressure, etc., or in the electric resistance of the skin, would represent processes of this kind. In all these cases, however, emotional changes in the subject exercise a disturbing influence, and it is almost impossible in practice to rule these out.

The tests for fatigue, devised and used in the laboratory, even if they were wholly reliable and satisfactory, are not available to any extent for the testing of fatigue under the conditions of practical work in the factory, yard, or office.

[1] Ash, *op. cit.*, and Drever, 'A New Test for Fatigue,' in *Child Study*, vol. IX.

The reasons vary in individual cases, but there is one reason which applies to all. If work is interrupted at various times and a test interpolated, there is certain to be some change of interest on the part of the subject in passing from his ordinary work to the test, and this change, whether favourable or unfavourable to the test itself, will in either case impair its value as a criterion of fatigue.

Practically when we are dealing with industrial work our main criterion for the presence or absence of fatigue must be the quantity and quality of the output for equal intervals of time at different periods of the day or week. In using this criterion we must discount the other factors upon which output depends. Independently of fatigue, constancy of output for equal intervals of time is not the normal condition, as we have already seen in our discussion of the work curve. Any attempt on the part of the management to compel the work in a factory to adapt itself rigidly to the principle of equal output for equal intervals of time will necessarily involve either slacking at times or 'sweating' at times, or both. Used judiciously, however, the quantity of output, or the amount of 'spoiled work', or both, is the best practical criterion we have in ordinary industrial work.

Another practical method, available in some industries, is the amount of machine power used per hour. It has also been claimed that the number of accidents is an index of the degree of fatigue in the workers. It is said, for example, that twenty-five per cent of the accidents which happen to dock-workers in London docks occur between 11 and 12 in the forenoon and between 3 and 4 in the afternoon. These are the times when we should expect the fatigue effects to be greatest. In the ordinary factory so many other things must be taken into account as determining causes of accidents that it is difficult to say how far the number of accidents can be taken as a reliable index of fatigue. From what we know of fatigue we should certainly expect the closest connexion between fatigue and accidents, and if we find that diminution in output is accompanied by increase in the number of accidents, we have almost conclusive evidence of a degree of fatigue which should not be permitted to be present, as a main contributory cause to both results.

One main point remains for consideration. That is the way in which the effects of fatigue can be eliminated or reduced. Of course the natural cure for fatigue is rest. There is, however, a popular idea that change of work is equivalent to rest. How far is the belief in accordance with fact? If there is real and pronounced central or general fatigue, the belief is not in accordance with fact at all. Any work whatever will simply increase such fatigue. If, however, the fatigue is in the main local fatigue, the fatigue mainly of a certain mechanism, then there can be no doubt that the activity of a different mechanism will allow the first to recover, and will so far eliminate the fatigue. On the other hand it must be noted that there is no local fatigue without some measure of central fatigue. Hence there will be a limit beyond which no change of work will lessen fatigue. Again, if, as is frequently the case, the change is made to work demanding less exertion, and therefore involving less consumption of energy-producing material and less accumulation of waste products, the onset of general fatigue may be considerably postponed.

The 'boredom' or 'weariness' arising from monotonous or otherwise uninteresting work is a particular case deserving of some notice. Now 'boredom', though itself not fatigue, simulates in its effects central fatigue. Not only so, but if work must be maintained in spite of 'boredom', there is rapid onset of central fatigue in its worst form. On the other hand this is a case where change of work is most helpful. The wise manager will take advantage of the fact. 'Boredom' is too harmful in its effects to be ignored.

Myers has drawn attention to the way the daily curve of output varies for different kinds of work. For strenuous muscular work, he says, we get a rapid and early rise followed by a definite fall in the morning spell, and then a recovery after dinner followed by a progressive fall. With work requiring skill and dexterity the rise is more gradual, and the fall less obvious in the morning, with a less complete recovery and a much smaller fall in the afternoon. In machine work the output reaches its maximum about the third hour in the morning spell, and then falls slightly, while in the afternoon a high level is maintained. In machine work where 'the factor of rhythmic action' is involved, output starts at a low level, increases enormously during the first three hours, then falls slightly, and in the afternoon the output remains high, often without any fall in the last hour.[1] Obviously, therefore, the onset of fatigue is different for different kinds of work, and so far each kind of work will require its own special treatment. The most effective method of reducing the fatigue effect is by an appropriate arrangement and distribution of work and rest periods. That method we must leave over for discussion in the next chapter.

Nature's own rest cure is sleep. Unless a sufficiency of sound and restful sleep is obtained, more or less central fatigue will be always present. The efficiency of industrial work will therefore depend to a considerable extent on the conditions under which the worker obtains his nightly sleep. From the other side efficiency of work depends on sufficiency of energy-producing material. This is obtained from food and fresh air. Hence the efficiency of industrial work will depend no less on the amount and quality of the food the worker eats, and the amount of fresh air he enjoys.

[1] *Mind and Work*, p. 62.

6

CHAPTER VIII

WORK AND REST PERIODS

IN the present chapter we must consider the practical significance for industry of a proper distribution of work and rest periods. We hope to show how important the results obtained by the physiologist and the psychologist in their investigation of work and fatigue are for the industrialist, the worker, and the practical man. To begin with, it will be well to give a brief résumé of the conclusions to which we are led by the results in question. Neglecting practice, which is only significant in the case of the 'new' hand, we have three factors determining the efficiency of work—warming up, settlement, and fatigue. Efficiency varies directly as the first two, inversely as the third. If the period of working is too short, efficiency will suffer from lack of the first two; if it is too long, efficiency will suffer because of the presence of the third.

The time that must elapse before work reaches its maximum efficiency will vary with the kind of work, with the environment, and with the individual worker; the time at which, and manner in which, fatigue shows itself will be similarly conditioned. The interposition of pauses at the proper intervals, and of the right length, will enable a high level of efficiency of work to be maintained. What are the right intervals, and what is the right length of pause, can be practically determined for the different kinds of work and for different individuals. Finally, there is a total length of daily work which will give the maximum of efficiency as measured in terms of output, and similarly, in those kinds of work to which it is applicable there is an optimal load. Again, these can be practically determined.

The influence of suitably distributed rests in promoting efficiency is admirably illustrated by a trench-digging competition, cited by Muscio, Myers, and others. Two squads of soldiers set out to try which could dig the greater number of yards of trench. The officer in command of the one party divided his men into three sections. Each section worked for five minutes at the top of their strength, then rested for ten minutes. There was thus only one section—a third of the men—working at a time. The officer in command of the other party used no definite system at all, but kept all his men working until they were tired out and had to take a rest. As soon as they seemed to be sufficiently rested, they resumed work as before. The result of the competition was an easy victory for the first group. This illustration is given here merely to emphasize the general fact. Other illustrations will be given in what follows, in order to show particular aspects of the general fact.

It may be laid down as a general principle that the more strenuous the work, the longer should the period of rest be relatively to the period of work. This is particularly applicable to the case of severe manual labour. Investigations carried out in the Bethlehem Steel Works in the case of men engaged in loading pig iron into railway trucks were held to show that the men should not be under the necessary load —92 lb.—for more than 43 per cent of the working day of nine hours, that is for a total time of $3\frac{3}{4}$ hours. The results of this piece of investigation are worth considering in detail. The men were specially selected for the work. They were kept working for periods of 7 minutes, and after each such period were required to rest for 10 minutes. They were instructed in the best manner of lifting the pigs of iron, and in the best rate of walking, with various other details of the work. The final result was an increase of 300 per cent in output—instead of a man lifting $12\frac{1}{2}$ tons per day, as under the old régime, he was now able to lift without any increase of fatigue an average of $47\frac{1}{2}$ tons. As a result of this there was a 66 per cent decrease in costs, and a 60 per cent increase in wages.

In all such cases it is evident that the question of load becomes an important one. With the loading of pig iron the load is fixed by the weight of each pig. Practically it may not be possible to alter the load. Sometimes, however, it is possible. An instance, which is important because of its wide applicability, is cited by Münsterberg and others. Again the locale was the Bethlehem Steel Works. Hundreds of men were employed in shovelling all kinds of material from heavy iron ore to light ashes. The same size of shovel was used in each case. The result was that with the heavy material the load was much too heavy, and fatigue developed rapidly, whereas with the light material the total work done was much less than it might have been, with no greater fatigue, but for the fact that the shovel would not take more at a time. Consequently the problem came to be to determine first the best working-load for a strong man, and to determine secondly the best arrangement of work and rest for that load. These problems having been solved, a special shovel was constructed for each kind of material, such that on an average the load would always be 21 lb., which was the optimal load determined. After regulating also in accordance with the results of experimental research the rate and movement in shovelling, the management found as the final outcome that 140 men could do the work previously requiring 500 men, that where the shovelling of 16 tons of material had previously been the average day's work, 59 tons on the average could now be shovelled. As a result the expenses for this type of work, inclusive of the expenses of the investigation and the increased cost of tools, were reduced by 50 per cent, and the wages of the shovellers increased by over 60 per cent.

These two investigations and their results raise a question of industrial policy which has its psychological aspect. What is to be the effect of increased output on employment? In the case last cited, where 140 men can do the work previously requiring 500, what is to happen to the other 360? The economist can show that ultimately increased output means not decreased but increased employment. The attitude of the individual worker, however, will be determined by immediate, not ultimate, results. The psychological fact, as distinct from the economic, is that you must convince the worker that he individually will not be the loser, and the trade union that its solidarity will not be imperilled. This difficulty can only be met by some effective system of guarantees against unemployment and loss during the transition period. What this system is to be it is hardly for the psychologist to discuss.

All the illustrations we have hitherto taken have been of heavy muscular work. The arrangement of rest pauses in all such cases must provide for relatively short work periods, or periods under load, and for relatively long rest periods. In the trench-digging competition, as the reader will remember, the rest period of the winning team was twice as long as the working period. The proportion changes as we come to deal with lighter muscular work, but of course the exact proportion between work and rest and the best arrangement of work and rest periods must be experimentally determined for each type of work. The work has already been done for particular kinds of work, but much remains to be done.

Two illustrations of the arrangements adopted in less strenuous muscular work may be given. Myers cites an instance in the bottle-making industry.[1] Three teams—each team consisted of a man and two boys—were employed for two machines. The working period was 40 minutes, and the employment of three teams instead of two enabled each team to have a rest of 20 minutes after 40 minutes' work, the machines being kept going continuously. The result was a considerable gain. The other instance is cited by Hollingworth and Poffenberger.[2] In this case the work was folding handkerchiefs. Every hour in the working day was divided into six-minute periods. Each six-minute period comprised five minutes' work and a one-minute rest. The result in this case was an increase in output of 200 per cent, though the workers were only actually working for five-sixths of the time.

With mental work, and probably highly skilled work of any kind, the period of warming-up and settlement tends to be somewhat long. Hence, if the efficiency is to be maintained at a high level, frequent rest pauses are undesirable.

[1] *Mind and Work*, p. 74.   [2] *Applied Psychology*, p. 151.

For mental work a five-minute rest at the end of each hour of work has been recommended. It is, however, very difficult to lay down definite schedules in such cases. Individual differences become more and more pronounced as we pass to this type of work, and must be more and more taken into account.

It cannot be too strongly urged that the mere arbitrary or capricious arrangement and distribution of work and rest periods cannot be expected to yield other than disappointing results. Any changes made should only be made after exhaustive experiment, and the experimental work required is such as the industrial psychologist is alone competent to carry out. Many well-meaning manufacturers and factory-managers have learned the truth of this from their own experience. Here once more is work waiting for the new profession of 'psychologist'.

The interposition of appropriate pauses in the day's work does not eliminate all fatigue. It merely retards its development to such extent as markedly to impair the working efficiency of the worker. The effect of the pause in maintaining efficiency at a high level is shown by the increase in output, even though the actual working time has been shortened. The elimination of fatigue, if it takes place at all, takes place in the rest period which intervenes between the work of one day and the work of the next. The solution, therefore, of the problem of so distributing work periods and rest periods as to secure maximum efficiency requires us to take account not only of the distribution of work and rest periods, and their length, in the day's work, but of the total length of the working day itself, its relation to the resting period before the work of the next day begins, and the various things that normally occupy this resting period in the life of the worker. That is to say, the psychologist has still another wide field of study and research to explore. Some of the work here also has been done, but very much remains to do.

It may sound somewhat paradoxical to say that a man may do more work in eight hours than he can do in nine hours.

But it must be remembered that work in an industrial undertaking goes on day after day, and week after week, and it may very well happen that a higher efficiency of work is maintained with the smaller number of hours per day to such an extent as to increase total output. From the results of laboratory investigations of work and fatigue we should, in fact, expect to find that there is an optimal length of working period per day which will yield the most efficient work and the greatest output, and that output and efficiency are both diminished either by working less or by working more. Hence it need not surprise us to find that in certain cases where it has been tried decrease in working hours has led to increase in output. Even where there has been no increase in output there has often been a decided gain in other respects, as in diminished amount of spoiled work diminished loss through sickness, bad time-keeping, and the like.

An admirable illustration of what may happen is given by Muscio and quoted by Myers.[1] An urgent order was received by two apple-growing estates managed by two brothers. The workers were paid on the piece-rate system. One of the brothers kept his men working at the ordinary number of hours per day—eight. In the other case the workers asked to be allowed to work overtime, and worked ten hours a day. At the end of a week the workers working eight hours a day were found to have averaged from five to six cases more per day than the workers working ten hours a day. Surely no more striking demonstration could be given of the fact that overtime is sometimes highly uneconomical, and may defeat its own end. There can be no doubt whatever that working overtime tends to make the worker put less energy into his work, sometimes consciously, sometimes unconsciously, as Myers points out, and as a sort of 'defence mechanism' on the part of the organism against excessive hours. It is of course not surprising that the piece-rate worker should be opposed to a shortening of hours until he is satisfied that his pay will not suffer, and that he will not be over-driven in

[1] *Lectures on Industrial Psychology*, and *Mind and Work*.

securing this result. With reasonable care and tact it should not be difficult to convince him of the facts. When pauses were introduced into some of our munition factories working on the piece-rate system, the same difficulty was experienced, but it disappeared before the fact of increased output.

Many illuminating results were obtained in our munition factories during the First World War from the various re-arrangements of working hours which took place at different times. None are more illuminating that the results of reducing the daily hours. In one case, that of men engaged in sizing fuses, the hours wrought per week were reduced from 58 to 50. The reduction was followed by an increase of 39 per cent in hourly output, and an increase of 21 per cent in total output. In another case—this time the case of women workers turning fuse bodies—the weekly hours were reduced from 66 to 48. This was followed by an increase of 68 per cent in hourly output, and of 15 per cent in total output.

Stanley Kent cites a case where a woman worker in a factory for surgical dressings refused to work overtime with the others from 6 to 8 in the evening, and also before breakfast from 6 to 8 in the morning. She asserted that she could do more work in the remaining eight hours worked than if she worked for the twelve hours with the others. Her claim was tested by comparing her output for a month with the output of other hands. Three first-class hands were selected, who worked twelve hours a day during the first fortnight, and ten hours a day during the rest of the month. Although she stayed away one whole day and three half-days during the month, the output of the 'slacker' for the period was 52,429 bobbins, against the best output of the others, 51,641, and an average output of the others of 48,529. She had worked 160 hours against their 237.[1]

The illustrations might easily be multiplied, but there is really no need. These facts speak for themselves, and the confirmation they give to experimental results obtained in the laboratory is absolute.

[1] *Engineering*, 6 October 1916.

There is one other important point to which Myers has drawn special attention.[1] That is that the full effects of reduced hours may not show themselves till after the lapse of a considerable period of time. The whole human system seems to have become adjusted to a certain rate of work and a certain period of work, and the new adjustment to the improved conditions is only 'gradually acquired. Further, there is an indication, though it cannot as yet be claimed that there is definite proof, that if, after the adjustment to the new conditions is established, the old working hours be reverted to, the output also immediately falls to the old rate. This fact, if it should prove to be a fact, must be taken into very serious consideration by those who would introduce over-time work on special occasions.

It is manifest that the effects of rests, both in the course of the day's work, and between the work of one day and the next, will depend a great deal on the manner in which the resting period is spent. This must be more particularly kept in mind in the case of the free time after the day's work is over. It is obvious that this time may be so harmfully employed as to more than balance the gain that should have accrued in the efficiency of the work. At this point industrial psychology touches the domain of social work, and to a still greater extent perhaps education. It is largely the business of the teacher to see that the gain, that might be derived from the application of psychology to industry in this respect, is not lost and even converted to the detriment of society.

[1] *Mind and Work*, p. 77.

CHAPTER IX

ECONOMY OF MOVEMENT AND METHOD IN LEARNING

PROBABLY no innovation of the scientific-management engineer has evoked more interest than his 'time and motion study'. He has opened a practically new field of investigation, and he has developed in this field a refinement of method and technique reminiscent of the psychological laboratory. But it is not the refinement of method that has interested the lay mind so much as the obvious importance of the study from the point of view of efficiency, and the extraordinarily wide scope for its application. All the mechanical improvements of the last few generations—and such improvements have been one of the most striking characteristics of that period in the history of mankind—have been improvements because they involved an economizing of energy or a saving of time, or both. The attempt to save time and economize energy in the movements of the worker is merely an extension to the human factor of the same principle, and ought, in precisely the same way and in proportion to the measure in which the movements of the worker play a significant part in the total outcome, to promote efficiency. Not only so, but there are numberless phases and directions of human labour, in which the mechanical element plays practically no part or only an insignificant one, which will be equally affected by this new development. From the housekeeper to the factory worker, from the navvy to the skilled mechanic, there is no branch of human labour involving the movement factor that is not interested.

An exceedingly good illustration of the wide range of significance attaching to movement study is given by Christine Frederick in her book *The New Housekeeping*.

'I recall a young bride,' she says, 'who recently showed

me her new kitchen. "Isn't it a beauty?" she exclaimed. It certainly had modern appliances of every kind. But her stove was in a recess of the kitchen at one end. Her pantry was twenty feet away at the opposite end. Every time she wanted to use a frying-pan she had to walk twenty feet to get it, and, after using it, she had to walk twenty feet to put it away. . . . When I see such a kitchen I am reminded of the barker I once heard outside of a country circus. "Ladies and gentlemen," he was calling, "come in and see the great African crocodile. It measures 18 feet from the tip of its nose to the tip of its tail, and 18 feet from the tip of its tail to the tip of its nose, making in all, ladies and gentlemen, a grand total of 36 feet." How many women are "making a grand total of thirty-six steps" every time they hang up the egg-beater?[1]

The practical aim of the scientific-management engineer in his study of movement was to find a way of saving the time and diminishing the fatigue of the worker, by eliminating all unnecessary movements, or by substituting easier, more effective, and more rapid movements for comparatively inefficient ones. We might therefore say that he had before him what may be described as a general problem and a problem of detail. All manual work consists of a series of movements. If, on the one hand, we can reduce the number of movements made in performing a task, we ought by so doing to expedite the performance of the task, provided the movements remaining are not prejudicially affected as regards time or difficulty. This is obvious, since no movement, however short and however rapid, can be performed in no time at all, and the elimination of any movement, under the conditions mentioned, must save the time that movement occupied, with the energy spent in the movement as well. The amount of saving will be in proportion to the time and energy spent in the movement which has been eliminated. A similar result will, on the other hand, be produced by the substitution of more efficient for less efficient individual

[1] *Op. cit.*, p. 46.

movements. The general problem in the study of movement is to effect a saving of time and energy in the first way; the problem of detail is to effect a saving in the second way. We shall consider them in turn. Analogues of both are of course to be found on the mechanical side of industry.

What may be done in the solution of the general problem, that is in the reduction of the number of necessary movements in any complex series of movements, is best illustrated by F. B. Gilbreth's well-known bricklaying experiment. This illustrates at one and the same time the elimination of wholly useless movements, as well as the obviating of movements by various simple devices by which the movements are rendered unnecessary. It is therefore worth describing in some detail.[1]

In the method of bricklaying as ordinarily practised *eighteen* separate movements were involved. Some of the movements were obviously unnecessary, and could easily be eliminated. The pile of bricks from which the worker took the bricks to be laid was at such a distance that he had to take a step to it for each brick, and a step back to the wall he was building to lay the brick. It was easy to place the pile nearer him so that these steps should not be necessary. Other movements were eliminated by being made unnecessary in other ways. For example, bricks and mortar were placed in such a position that the worker did not require to bend to the level of his feet, a very fatiguing movement in any case. This change was effected by the introduction of a table to carry the bricks and mortar. The successive picking up of the brick and the trowel of mortar was replaced by the simultaneous picking-up with one movement of the brick with the left hand and the trowel of mortar with the right. The tap with the trowel which the bricklayer gave each brick after laying it was replaced by a slight pressure on the brick as it was laid. Finally, it was customary for the brick-layer to inspect each brick to see that it was placed with the proper face outwards, and if necessary to turn it. The inspection, act of volition, and turning of the brick were

[1] Quoted by several writers: Taylor, Münsterberg, Muscio, etc.

eliminated by making it the duty of a special man—unskilled —to see that the bricks were placed on the table in such a way that the bricklayer—the skilled man—could place them immediately on the wall without turning them. The result of all this was that the necessary movements were reduced to *five*, and that by the new method a bricklayer was able to lay 350 bricks per hour, in place of the 120 which represented the normal hour's work on the old method.

Further illustrations might easily be given, but this ought to suffice as far as the general problem is concerned. In this bricklaying experiment two important principles are exemplified, by which a saving is effected in time and energy, which have little to do with 'motion study' in the strict sense in which it is now generally used. The first of these principles is the principle of so arranging tools and materials as to enable each to be taken at the proper time for its use, without any needless waste of time and energy. The second is the principle of economizing the time and energy of the highly skilled workman by using the time and energy of the unskilled for performing such functions as the unskilled can easily perform. Both are important principles, and in practice they tend to produce the result at which the study of movement was aiming from the beginning.

'Motion study' as now understood, that is the study of the actual movements made, aims at the same result, and seeks to attain that result by substituting, as we have said, more efficient for less efficient movements and movement elements. This involves a study of each particular movement in detail. The history of the development of methods of detailed 'motion study' is full of interest. At first the experimenter merely watched the movement, with a stop-watch in hand, and recorded the time taken. It was found that the 'same' movement—as far as the purpose and intention of the worker was concerned—was made by two different workers in very different times. At least we may suppose this to have been the finding. The real problem had then to be faced of determining the reasons why this difference of time existed. Once the reasons for the difference were discovered, the elimination of the difference was a practical question which might be met in one of two practical ways, either by teaching the inferior workman the better movement, or, if that were impossible, using the time of movement as a test for selecting workers for that particular work.

It was soon discovered that in this kind of investigation the method employed, of observing the movement with stop-watch in hand, was not nearly sufficiently delicate, was in fact quite inadequate for dealing with such a problem. The next step was to get a photographic record of the movement as made by different individuals, which would show what differences, if any, there were in the actual elements of which the movement as a whole was built up. A photograph was obtained by attaching a small electric lamp to the moving limb, and placing a camera in such a way that the moving light would trace a line on the exposed plate. The timing of the whole movement was still done with the stop-watch. A simple mechanical device, however, could be adopted, which would enable the experimenter to dispense with the stop-watch. This was the next step taken. It consisted in the introduction into the circuit of the electric lamp of an interrupter which would interrupt the current supplying the lamp at regular intervals. The result of this was to produce on the camera plate a series of dashes, in place of a continuous line, each dash representing a known interval of time. This is the arrangement known as the *chronocyclegraph*.

Two other refinements have been added. In order to show in which direction the movement is taking place, an ingenious arrangement is made, by which the current is interrupted gradually, in place of being cut off at once. The effect of this is to substitute on the photographic plate blunt arrowheads for dashes. In order to measure the exact extent of any movement, steps are taken to secure that the photograph of a screen showing squares of known dimensions is introduced on the same plate as, and underlying, the photograph of the movement. For some purposes this last appears a rather unnecessary refinement, since simple measurement and a constant distance would seem to serve the same end. It ought to be mentioned that cinematography has also been employed, the face of a clock being recorded on the film for timing purposes.

In the way described, a photographic record of any movement may be obtained, from which time, extent, and direction of movement may be directly read off. But the record is on a plane surface, and the actual movement may involve space of three dimensions. So far, the photograph will apparently be a rather imperfect representation of the movement for purposes of 'motion study'. This difficulty is got over by employing a stereoscopic camera. By means of this we get two photographs, which on being placed in a stereoscope enable us to see the movement in tridimensional space. The record of the movement is thus complete. To allow the movement to be studied carefully and in detail at his leisure, the investigator now constructs from this stereoscopic view a wire model in three dimensions. Working from this model, he determines where and how modifications can be introduced, which will have the effect of shortening the path of movement. The only thing remaining is to determine practically whether this effect can be realized, and then the 'motion study' has attained its end.

Most of this development in the methods of detailed 'motion study' has been the work of F. B. and L. M. Gilbreth. The culmination of their work in this field is represented by their process chart, or, as they call it, 'simo-chart'. In this chart an analysis is made of a piece of work into the ultimate movement units, called 'therbligs' (Gilbreth inverted). A fairly elaborate system of symbols is employed to indicate the actual movement performed, as 'search', 'find', select', 'grasp', etc., and a standardized colour scheme to enable the observer to pick out, and study with greater facility, the different movements, with the time taken in each case. This colour record is presented vertically, and the parts of the body involved are noted horizontally. Psychologists tend to become very critical of the theory underlying these refinements. The objective is to find 'the one best way' of carrying out a piece of work. The method of finding this 'one best way' is to study by the various detailed methods developed by the Gilbreths, the simo-charts of skilled workers, select the quickest movements at each stage, and construct, by combining these, a movement form, which is to be taught to all new employees as the 'one best way' of doing the work. The theory underlying this procedure is quite unacceptable to most psychologists. The smooth, rhythmical flow of a skilled movement is not attained initially by piecing together the elements in this way, and cannot be so attained. The quickest movement, that is, the one requiring the shortest time, is not necessarily the easiest and least fatiguing. Each skilled worker has his own individual characteristics, physical and psychological, and the skilled movements express these characteristics in an individual, and probably unique, way. These are some of the objections, which, with some justice, have been urged. On broader grounds it is objected that the dehumanizing and mechanizing of the human being, which tends to result from forcing this 'one best way' on every worker, is itself very undesirable, and, in the long run, does not pay, from an economic and social point of view.

To prevent the reader getting a wrong impression, it is necessary to say that time has still to show whether all these refinements in 'motion study' are justified by results. That 'motion study' itself is justified by results is unquestionable. Some illustrations may be given. These are selected mainly from Myers.[1] An operation in moulding normally took 53 minutes. The investigator said that, if the workers were trained in improved methods, it should be done in 44 minutes. Actually, after the workmen had become expert through practice, it was done in 20 minutes. This meant an increase of 165 per cent in output, and the wages of the men were as a result increased by 60 per cent. In a case of cotton folding, the separate movements were reduced from 20–30 to 10–12. This involved an increase in output of 220 per cent. In the work of putting paper covers on small boxes there was an increase of output amounting to 100 per cent.

[1] *Mind and Work*, pp. 13–16.

The same result was obtained in a sweets factory. An increase of output amounting to 170 per cent was obtained in packing cloth, and of 230 per cent in pillow-case making.

But in these and other results achieved by 'motion study' there is another important psychological factor to be taken into account, which as yet has merely been indicated. It is not sufficient for the expert investigator to discover more efficient movements and better methods. The worker must also be trained in these new movements and methods. Hence efficiency of movement as a problem for the industrial psychologist is practically bound up with the further problem of economy in learning. Our next task is, therefore, to consider the psychological phenomena of learning, so far as these have a bearing upon the present problems.

There are two groups of phenomena investigated by the psychology of learning, which seem specially relevant to the industrial problems and needs at this point. These are the phenomena of interference, already discussed in a previous chapter,[1] and the phenomena of distribution of repetitions or of learning periods. The phenomena of interference do not require to be described again. They come into the picture here, because of the fact that a wrong or imperfect movement made by a workman in learning any new movement, tends to delay and retard the learning, and may in extreme cases impair the efficiency of the workman permanently as far as that movement is concerned. Hence in some cases it may be easier to teach a new movement to a novice than to a man who has become expert in the movement we wish to replace. This in itself may explain the opposition which a reform of this kind frequently meets on the part of the worker. The opposition may be in the nature of a 'defence mechanism' against a more or less unconscious anticipation of the difficulty or the inferiority the change is likely to involve. But the most important lesson which the psychology of learning inculcates in this connexion is the

[1] Chapter VI. For fuller discussion see author's *Psychology of Everyday Life*.

desirability of careful supervision at the start of practice to prevent a wrong movement being acquired early. Not only does the wrong movement impair efficiency through interference because it is the wrong movement, but the older it is, that is the earlier it is acquired, the more permanent is its effect. This means, of course, that mistakes made at a late stage in the process of learning a new movement are far less significant and serious, as far as the impeding of the learning itself is concerned, than mistakes made at an early stage. All sorts of practical rules could be deduced, but that which contains them all is, 'Make sure that the movement is right from the start'.

Of the many experimental investigations of learning, few have brought to light results of greater practical importance, in a great variety of fields, than those bearing upon the distribution of learning periods. It has been shown that in learning something by heart a given number of repetitions will produce a better effect the more widely they are distributed. Suppose, for example, that we intend to give twelve repetitions. We shall get the poorest result from these repetitions by taking them one after another at a single sitting, and the best result by taking them one a day for twelve successive days. The case of practice or learning periods is more or less analogous. There are limits to the economical distribution of repetitions or practice, but these limits depend on the conditions which rule efficiency or work rather than on learning itself. An American investigator, Starch, using the 'substitution test' for the learning, compared four groups of subjects, working with different learning periods. The first groups worked 10 minutes at a time twice a day for six days; the second group worked 20 minutes at a time once a day for six days; the third group worked 40 minutes at a time every other day for six days; and the fourth group worked right on for 120 minutes at a single sitting. Each subject made a mark at the end of every five minutes of work to show the point he had reached. The results showed that the shorter and more numerous the intervals, the more rapid was the improvement. But the curves of learning also showed that the limit of economical learning had nearly been reached, if it had not been over-stepped. The advantage of the 10-minute group over the 20-minute group was much less than the advantage of the latter over the 40-minute group, and at one point, late in the learning, the curve for the 20-minute group crossed and ran above the curve for the 10-minute group. It is interesting to note that the shorter period gave an advantage from the outset, even during the first ten minutes of work, when one might suppose that all the groups would be equal. This was probably due to the fact that this group unconsciously put more energy into their work, and would from that point of view indicate a further cause of increased efficiency of work when pauses are duly distributed.

There can be little doubt that a great deal of the time we spend in the practice of various things—games and the like—is spent very uneconomically from the point of view of acquiring that skill which is the aim of the practice. The same holds of work. In Starch's experiment, if we represent the efficiency of the first group after two hours' practice by 300, the efficiency of the fourth group would be only 140 after the same period of practice. The difference is a very significant one, and indicates with sufficient clearness the extent of the loss in time which a bad distribution of practice periods may involve. The best distribution of practice periods will doubtless depend on a variety of circumstances, and there is need for more investigation here, especially investigation bearing upon the different kinds of practice, or rather of skill, involved in industrial work, but the general principle is clear.

The effect of the distribution of learning periods on the acquirement of skill depends in part on the factors determining efficiency of work, which have already been discussed in the last chapter. But it depends also in part on interference. The influence of interfering wrong associations and connexions is eliminated by allowing a period of time to elapse. Working with mirror-drawing—that is drawing by watching the hand and the figure in a mirror in place of directly—as a practical exercise in the study of learning, with the students in the laboratory, we often get results of this kind: the student makes, say, six attempts, and acquiring skill with the practice succeeds in reducing the time taken to trace a simple figure from about four minutes at the first attempt to about a minute and a half at the sixth; then when he tries again after a fortnight, without having any practice during the intervening time, his time at the first trial may have dropped to seventy-five seconds. An American investigator in a typewriting experiment extending over five years, tested a subject four and a half months, and again a year and a half after he had had practice. On the first occasion the score was slightly lower than the average of the last ten of the practice series, but in the second and later test a decided gain on these practice results was shown.

One other point about learning deserves to be noted. Where a process of learning is extended over a long period of practice, the curve of learning does not show a continuous gain in skill or dexterity. It shows rather a series of slopes with intervening plateaus, and this seems to be a characteristic of all learning. The explanation appears to be that in any complex learning process habits of different orders or levels must be established. The lower-order habits must be established before it is possible to advance to the acquiring of higher-order habits. Any attempt to advance too quickly will defeat itself. A knowledge of this fact is important for any one who has to supervise training. It enables him, on the one hand, to give encouragement where it is needed because of apparent lack of progress, and on the other hand to prevent the learner trying to go too fast, and so running the risk of losing much of what he has gained. In the phenomenon of the 'plateau' interference also seems to play a prominent part. The acquiring of higher co-ordinations is only possible when the lower co-ordinations have been established. The reason is that the two orders of habits or co-ordinations interfere with one another, unless the first has been completely established and so made mechanical before the learning of the second starts. There is mutual interference. Hence the attempt to go too quickly may lose much of what has already been acquired.

These facts and phenomena of learning have obviously a much wider application than merely to the results of 'motion study'. Every industrial undertaking must at all times reckon on a certain proportion of its employess being 'new' hands. Even when the traditional movements and traditional methods of work are retained, the 'new' hands have to learn these movements and methods of work. Haphazard learning of the kind which has hitherto prevailed is attended with considerable risk, and may easily prove very expensive. The risk is that, as a result of wrong learning, the efficiency of a workman may be permanently impaired. The expense is incurred by the waste of time, energy, and possibly material, which uneconomical learning involves. The greater the extent to which the process to be learned demands high technical skill, the more serious the risk and the waste attending haphazard learning. Hence expenditure on the systematic organization of learning in all industries, and the systematic application of the psychological principals underlying learning, will, beyond question, repay itself with interest, both to the individual employer and to the community at large, in the increased efficiency of work which will result. This is partly an argument for technical schools, but it is difficult to believe that technical schools can meet all the needs of industry in this regard.

CHAPTER X

OTHER FACTORS INFLUENCING EFFICIENCY OF WORK

THE other main factors which may play a part in determining the worker's efficiency may be gathered together and briefly discussed in a single chapter. They fall into two groups—a group which we may characterize as physiological rather than psychological, in its direct action, and a group which is primarily psychological. In the first group would come the lighting, ventilation, and temperature of the workshop or factory; in the second group the chief factors are the presence or absence of distraction in the conditions under which the work must be done, and the emotional state of the worker. To some extent the separation of the factors in this way is arbitrary, as we shall see presently, but they may be discussed in the order in which we have named them.

LIGHTING

Some interesting and industrially important work has been done in recent times on the effects of various intensities and kinds of illumination on the worker in school or home, office, or factory. We tend to be somewhat incredulous regarding the alleged effects of good and bad lighting respectively on the efficiency of work, until the *modus operandi* of the physical stimulus, and the physiological and psychological phenomena involved, become clear to us. These phenomena are of four distinct kinds. In the first place a bright object, like an electric light, or its reflection on a highly polished surface, coming into the margin of the field of vision, tends to draw the attention and the eye towards it. This tendency is a reflex or instinctive tendency operating independently of our volition. The light strikes on the margin of the retina, and the eye immediately turns towards it so as to bring it into the field of direct vision. The movement of the eye is produced by the contraction of certain muscles. In order to prevent its taking place the antagonistic muscles must be kept in a state of tension. Hence the worker, who is attending to, and fixing his eyes upon some object directly in front of him, at which he is working, will have to exercise muscular energy continuously to maintain this fixation, provided there is a bright light stimulating the margin of the retina at the same time. There will thus be consumption of energy, and naturally, therefore, an earlier onset of fatigue, and to a by no means insignificant extent. In the second place there is also an instinctive tendency of focus the eye for the bright object in the marginal field which is attracting attention. This also is done by means of muscular contraction, and its resistance involves the consumption of energy. In the third place the margin of the retina, and not the centre, is most sensitive to light intensity. In very dim light the centre is practically blind, and it is by means of the marginal field that we see. As adjusted for dim light, the marginal field is always highly sensitive to light intensity; as adjusted for bright light, the centre of the visual field is not highly sensitive. Bright light, therefore, falling on the marginal field, say from the side, always produces an uncomfortable glare. Apart from the permanent injurious effect on the eyesight, the immediate effect, the discomfort, is highly distracting and deleterious as far as efficiency of work is concerned. In the fourth place, in consequence of the phenomena of visual contrast, if two neighbouring retinal areas are stimulated with very different light intensities, as in the case of high lights and deep shadows, both light and shadow will be enhanced, with the result that even a moderately bright light may produce an uncomfortable glare.

The main practical deduction from all this is the importance of uniformity of illumination. Uniformity is much more important than intensity under actual working conditions in the factory. Within limits the eye can adapt itself to a light of lower intensity without any loss in efficiency, except for very special kinds of work demanding high light intensity. With daylight it is much easier to get the best conditions of illumination realized, though even with daylight the wrong location of the windows relative to the workers, and lack of care in removing polished surfaces, dark shades, and the like out of the visual field may neutralize all the advantages. Where artificial lighting must be resorted to, naked lights should be avoided. Indirect lighting will obviously be the most satisfactory. But there does not seem any need to enter into details. After what has been said, the principles upon which efficient lighting will in the main depend, ought to be quite clear. Muscio states[1] that 'a certain firm increased the output of its evening workers ten per cent, simply by changing its system of lighting'.

TEMPERATURE AND VENTILATION

Recent years have seen a great increase in our knowledge of the facts and phenomena of ventilation, very largely through the systematic experimental investigations conducted in the laboratories of the New York State Commission on Ventilation. It has been clearly shown that many of the traditional views regarding the need for ventilation, the real producing causes of the bad effects arising from lack of ventilation and the like, were erroneous, or at any rate require considerable modification. Thus it was formerly believed that the lassitude and headache experienced by an individual confined in a crowded and badly ventilated room were due to the decrease of oxygen and increase of carbon dioxide in the confined air, which resulted from the fact that the individuals in the room, in breathing, exhausted the oxygen and breathed out carbon dioxide. Now, there cannot be any doubt that the decrease of oxygen and increase of carbon dioxide in the air of a room, provided it exceeded certain limits, would produce deleterious effects. But as far as physiological experiments go, no such effects can be demonstrated, until the decrease and increase are far beyond the limits actually found in the worst ventilated schools or factories. It has also been supposed that organic matter given off from the lungs and from the surface of the human

[1] *Lectures on Industrial Psychology*, 2nd ed., p. 161.

body contains a poison called 'anthropotoxin', which is the producing cause of the various bad effects. This theory must also be abandoned. Experiments on animals, which were supposed to support it, have been shown to have been unsatisfactory and inconclusive, and the technique of the experiments faulty.

It can now be regarded as certain that it is the rise of body temperature, and not the contaminated air, that brings about the discomfort, lassitude, and headache, experienced in a badly ventilated room, and that the rise of body temperature is determined by increase of temperature and humidity in the enclosed space. The body itself under ordinary conditions produces more heat than is necessary for the maintenance of the normal temperature, and to an extent in proportion to the degree of muscular, glandular, and nervous activity. This excess heat is given off mainly by radiation from the surface of the body, and evaporation of the perspiration. Obviously with rise of temperature of the surrounding air the radiation will tend to diminish, and if the temperature rises beyond a certain point it will cease altogether, and radiation in the opposite direction take its place. The balance may for some time be preserved by increased perspiration and evaporation. But with increase in the humidity of the surrounding air, evaporation from the body surface will tend proportionately to be retarded. The result of both these changes will therefore be to raise the body temperature above the normal, and the condition will become that of 'fever'. With poor ventilation this is precisely what takes place. The temperature of the air gradually rises, and at the same time the air becomes saturated with moisture, and its cooling effect on the body disappears. The continuous displacing of heated and saturated by fresh air through ventilation prevents the development of the injurious condition.

That this is the real explanation of what happens can be conclusively demonstrated by experiment. If several individuals are kept for some time in an air-tight chamber, they begin to show the usual familiar symptoms of bad ventilation. These symptoms do not disappear even if they are allowed to breathe fresh air by means of tubes extending into the outer air. An individual in the outer air, breathing through a tube the air of the chamber, does not show the symptoms. Hence obviously it is the being in the room atmosphere, not the breathing of it, that produces the symptoms.

The chief practical conclusions to be drawn from the facts as they are now known are: (1) that too high a temperature should not be maintained in houses, workshops, or factories, and (2) that enclosed air should be kept in motion by fans or by a current of air from open windows. The temperature of factory or workshop should be maintained between 50 and 60 degrees Fahrenheit, tending towards the lower or the upper limit according as the workers are vigorously or moderately active. The optimal humidity varies with the temperature. The higher the temperature the more moisture can the air hold. If the humidity is too low the effect will be dry and sore throat. At the temperatures recommended the wet bulb thermometer ought to read about 7 degrees below the dry bulb.

The effect of good or bad conditions with respect to ventilation on working efficiency is both direct and indirect, both physiological and psychological. Experiments show that the impairment of physical efficiency may be considerable. Thus it has been shown that the physical efficiency at a temperature of 68 degrees is 37 per cent greater than it is at 86 degrees. The mental effect is more complex and not so easily determined. Apparently no immediate impairment of mental efficiency may take place even when the conditions are extremely adverse as far as physical efficiency is concerned. Experimental work on these problems, however, is still being carried on.

Another factor affecting efficiency of work, to which scientific-management engineers have devoted some attention recently, is the position which must be maintained by the worker during working-time. If the worker has to stand for a long period, or maintain a cramped position, it is obvious that the total fatigue produced is only partly due to the work.

Provided these additional fatigue-producing agencies are eliminated, the work ought to gain in efficiency. In view of this various devices have been introduced to enable the worker to sit, or at least keep a half-sitting position, during work. Some of these devices are interesting from the point of view of industrial management and welfare work, but they involve no new psychological principles.

DISTRACTION

The experimental evidence with respect to the influence of distraction on the efficiency of work is very conflicting, and very difficult to interpret. This statement may appear surprising to a person who has never conducted such experiments, and is unacquainted with experimental results obtained by others. It seems so obvious that distraction must impair the efficiency of work, when we think of the effect on our own work of an aching tooth or a throbbing finger. If it does not immediately and directly impair working efficiency, it must surely accelerate the onset of fatigue. That is what might be called the view of the layman. But a little experience in the experimental investigation of the effects of distraction will soon dispel the confident notion that we already know all about it. The author has conducted a fairly extensive series of experiments on schoolchildren, varying in age from eight to fourteen, with the object of determining the effect on efficiency of work of distraction by noise, and on adults, using electric shocks in place of noise. In the children experiments the character of the noises was changed every half-minute to prevent accommodation taking place, and in some cases the intensity was sufficiently great to compel the head master of the school to remove from his room, which adjoined that in which the experiments were conducted, because he could not get on with his correspondence. The work done by the children was the cancellation of the A's in a specially prepared blank. Though the results varied in detail with children of different ages, the output of work almost uniformly showed increase, without any deterioration in quality, under the distraction. In the experiments with adults cancellation was also employed, but in this case of all the vowels in a column of ordinary newspaper print. The electric shocks were given to the left hand, the right hand being employed in the cancellation. While it was possible to increase the intensity of the shocks so as to inhibit work altogether with some subjects, when the intensity was kept moderate the same results with respect to quantity and quality of output were obtained as in the experiments with the children. It ought to be said that in both cases steps were taken to eliminate any effect due to practice and warming-up.[1]

There are two possible explanations of such results. On the one hand, a voluntary call is made on reserves of energy which are not normally called upon. The motive for this call is something which might be described as 'pugnacity' or aggressiveness. It seems clear that this additional consumption of energy must in the end considerably accelerate the onset of fatigue. On the other hand, the stimulus of the distraction may heighten the energy of discharge involuntarily and unconsciously, in somewhat the same way as a flash of light falling simultaneously on the retina intensifies the knee-jerk. What the ultimate effect of this is likely to be under ordinary working conditions it is exceedingly difficult to say. Theoretically the additional consumption of energy ought to involve an earlier onset of fatigue; practically it is not at all certain that this result should be reckoned on.

It is highly probable that there are great individual differences in manner of responding to distractions, and that some people are very much more sensitive to distractions than others, that people are more sensitive at some times than at other times, that different people are sensitive to different kinds of distraction, that distractions which are simply stimulating to one person at one time may be a real discomfort to another or to the same person at another time. Where work must be done under distracting conditions, the right type of individual ought to be selected on the basis of vocational tests. It may be taken as certain that when there is a conscious

[1] Investigation unfinished and results not yet published.

battle against distracting influences, the consumption of energy is considerably in excess of that required by the work itself, and so far distracting influences should be reduced to a minimum. It is probable also that sensitivity to distraction varies with the kind of work on which the individual is engaged, and with the extent to which the particular distraction can be accommodated to by the organism. A continuous and regular loud noise is not necessarily highly distracting. As Münsterberg points out,[1] 'strong rhythmical sounds such as heavy hammer blows, which dominate the continuous noises' are much more serious distracting influences than the continuous noises themselves. They may force on the worker a continuous struggle between the external rhythm and the different rhythm of his work with a highly fatiguing effect. Münsterberg also records a case where the removal of a woman engaged in work demanding high concentration of attention from a busy and noisy part of a printing shop to a quiet corner brought about an increase of 25 per cent in her output.[2] The whole problem of distraction in industrial work is a very complex one, and demands much more complete and detailed investigation than has yet been given to it.

EMOTIONAL STATE

In a very valuable chapter on 'Industrial Unrest' in his book, *Mind and Work*, Myers had discussed some of the effects on industry which are dependent on the emotional state of the worker. The scope of his discussion is much wider than the topic we are concerned with at present. But it is obvious that all the factors to which he calls attention, as factors determining social and industrial unrest, must affect efficiency of work, either directly or indirectly by accelerating fatigue. Worry, discontent, irritation, and the like, should obviously as far as possible be eliminated by removal of the causes. We have already instanced the spirit of the football field as a spirit which, so far as practicable, is worth cultivating in the workshop or factory. The general emotional state, however, we must pass over with this brief

[1] *Psychology and Industrial Efficiency*, p. 211.   [2] *Op. cit.*, p. 210.

mention. What we wish more particularly to draw attention to is certain specific factors that exercise an influence on efficiency of work, as it were, through the emotional state which they determine.[1]

One factor is the emotional effect of rhythm. We might have discussed rhythm under the head of economy of movement, or under the head of fatigue, for there is no doubt that it is a method by which energy may be economized, and the onset of fatigue postponed, just because it is a method by which the strain of volitional attention and decision is lessened. But it is very questionable whether this is the main and significant effect. Rhythm always has what may be justly described as an emotional value, and it is largely because of this emotional value that it plays the part in activity which it has been shown to play. Monotony, which is a matter of the mental attitude rather than of the nature of the work, might be supposed to be at its maximum when regular rhythmical movement is maintained over a long period. Practically, however, the reverse happens, and this is without doubt due to the fact that rhythmical movement has a single, primitive, but none the less real and important, emotional value.

The emotional effect of rhythm has been utilized in work and in play from very early times, and is to-day utilized both among civilized and among primitive peoples. Poetry and music, the most adequate of all expressions of human emotion, depend largely upon the same ancient, deep-seated, and powerful principle of human nature. But this emotional effect no psychologist has yet satisfactorily explained. In the meantime the industrial psychologist must rest content with the knowledge that such a principle exists, and that work can be facilitated and made pleasant by due regard to the phenomena in which it manifests itself.

ACCIDENTS

Another factor is fear of accidents. Dangerous occupations are highly fatiguing, because they involve this powerful

[1] *See* Chapter VI.

distracting influence, and the overstrain which it engenders. There may be a certain measure of accommodation on the part of some individuals, but it is apparent rather than real, and usually very far from complete. The obvious practical deduction, from the point of view of efficiency, is that the workman should be guarded in every possible way against dangers which are inevitable, and dangers which are not inevitable should be removed. To put the matter on no higher grounds, such action would be economically profitable.

Safety measures against accidents, therefore, may be said to contribute to the efficiency of industry by relieving anxiety, and giving increased confidence to the workers. But recent investigations have shown that the psychologist has another interest in industrial accidents, and that the safety measures, based upon what we may call the physical conditions of the situation, by no means exhaust the possibilities of measures that may be taken for the prevention of accidents. The investigation of accidents from the physiological and psychological side, rather than the physical, from the side of the human being meeting with the accident, rather than the machine causing it, has led to the important conclusion that there are individual differences in susceptibility to accidents, which can to some extent be determined beforehand. As Viteles[1] puts it: 'Some individuals become more frequently involved in accidents than others because of either an inherent psycho-physiological predisposition towards accidents, or because of a temporary change in attitude or outlook which increases the probabilities of being involved in an accident when a situation which may lead to one arises.' Unfortunately also the trouble may not end with the accident-susceptible individual. His companions at work alongside him may be involved in an accident originating in his psycho-physical make-up, so that he may become unconsciously a menace in the factory, or other industrial undertaking.

One of the earliest statistical studies of individual liability to accidents was that made by Greenwood and Woods,

[1] *Op. cit.*, p. 334.

working under the Industrial Fatigue Research Board (now Industrial Health Research Board), and published as Report No. 4 in 1919. The authors investigated the distribution of industrial accidents among individuals, considering whether the statistical analysis of the distribution showed it to be a chance distribution, a biased distribution, or an 'unequal liability' distribution, and concluded that the distribution was definitely not a chance distribution, and that there was distinct evidence of differences in individual liability to accidents. A German investigator, Marbe, investigating distribution of accidents from the point of view of insurance risk, came to similar conclusions. To Marbe is due the formulation of the law known as 'Marbe's Law', to the effect that 'the probability that an individual will experience an accident can be determined from the number he has already incurred'.

Assuming that this susceptibility to accidents, or 'accident proneness', as it has usually, though not very happily, been designated, depends at least partly on individual psychological characteristics, other investigators, notably Farmer and Chambers[1] in this country, have sought to discover by means of testing, what these psychological characteristics are. Intelligence tests, temperament tests, and aesthetokinetic tests—that is tests of motor reaction to sensory stimuli or rather perception—were employed, and the results seemed to indicate that the last had definite value in predicting accident liability. The investigators also found that these same tests correlated fairly highly with efficiency in the particular jobs of the subjects tested. This would indicate that tests employed for selection purposes might also be used to bring out 'accident proneness', where the selection was for occupations in which the risk of accidents was significant.

[1] Industrial Fatigue Research Board Reports, Nos. 36 and 55.

CHAPTER XI

ADVERTISING AND DISPLAY

WE must now pass to the third group of problems, the problems of the market, the problems of the relation of buyer to seller, of manufacturer to consumer. Much psychological work has been done in this field in recent years. In fact the literature on the psychology of advertising itself is very extensive, more especially in America, where research and teaching in the psychology of advertising and salesmanship has developed on a scale that threatens serious rivalry with the psychology of education.

Buying and selling are usually regarded only from the economic standpoint, and we explain the process in terms of the economic laws of supply and demand. But if we look a little deeper, it is easy to see that the process is ultimately based on psychological rather than economic factors, for the demand is caused by felt human needs and wants, and the supply is of commodities for the satisfaction of such needs and wants. Moreover, the needs and wants must be understood psychologically, if they are to be understood at all. Some are original needs, needs characteristic of human nature as such, the needs for food, shelter, clothing, and the like. Others are acquired needs, and often vary considerably in character and in intensity with different classes and groups of human beings. A psychological understanding of the needs may be necessary, or at least highly desirable, for the manufacturer or seller, because of the fact that some of the needs can be modified easily, some resist any attempt at modification, some tend always to take precedence of others, some tend to seek satisfaction in a more or less habitual way, and so on. There are buying habits, and 'consumers' defences', and effective methods of appeal, all of which seriously concern the business man, and all of which depend wholly on psychological factors.

We have used the singular 'process' rather than the plural 'processes', because it is evident that we are concerned with only one economic process, which we call buying or selling according as we look at it from the one side or the other, however many psychological processes may be involved. Buying and selling are strictly correlative terms, in precisely the same way as teaching and learning are. No one can be said to sell unless some one buys, and similarly no one buys unless some one sells. The process must therefore be regarded as in the nature of a reaction between two individuals, the one who sells and the one who buys. There are various means by which the occurrence of this reaction is promoted—means on the side of the buyer, it may be, or on the side of the seller. Advertising is one such means on the side of the seller or the buyer, usually in the business world of the former. It represents action with the object of bringing on the reaction of buying and selling; and as this reaction is in the last analysis, as we have seen, a psychological reaction, the success of advertising depends almost wholly on psychological factors. The same is true of any other means that may be taken to promote the reaction. So obvious, however, are the psychological factors in the case of advertising, and so important are these factors in buying and selling generally, and in the business world at large, that it seems desirable to begin our discussion of the psychology of the market with a consideration of advertising. We may then consider other methods of bringing on the reaction under the head of 'display', and in the next chapter—and finally—the art of salesmanship itself.

We are assuming that advertising is done by one who wishes to become a seller, and that its object is to induce others to become buyers. Now prospective buyers fall into different classes, according to their psychological condition with respect to buying. Four such classes must be distinguished. First of all there is the individual who wishes to buy, and who has complete and definite knowledge of the exact thing he wishes to buy. Secondly there is the individual who wishes to buy, but only knows in a general kind of way the sort of thing that will meet his want. Thirdly there is the individual who has—if we may put it that way—money which he wishes to spend, but has only the vaguest idea with regard even to the kind of thing he will buy. Lastly there is the individual who is merely not unwilling to buy, not resolved not to buy. These prospective buyers may be designated A, B, C, and D; the would-be seller, who is advertising, we can call X. It must of course be assumed that A, B, C, and D all belong to the wide or narrow circle of people who would be likely to buy X's article or articles, and this class will be determined by various circumstances, all operating psychologically, according to the nature of the article in question. Obviously the problem which faces X is different in each case. Before considering the individual cases, however, we may profitably try to understand the ways in which advertising itself produces its effects, and the conditions under which the effects are produced.

The first effect which an advertisement produces, or is intended to produce, is the attracting of the attention. There are two general ways in which our attention may be attracted. The one way depends on the things we are interested in, and consists in an appeal to these interests. This kind of appeal for the attention is always of very great importance, and especially so in a case like that of B, where the interests are already strongly inclined in a certain direction; so important is it that a knowledge of general human psychology is probably even more important in business than a knowledge of the applied psychology of salesmanship and advertising. The second way is, however, more characteristic of the kind of appeal for attention that is usually made by the advertise-ment. It depends on the impression made on the senses. The vividness of an impression, the suddenness or unex-pectedness, its novelty—all tend to attract the attention. But one important qualification must be noted. Very few people read advertisements, after their attention has been attracted in this way, for the mere pleasure of reading them. Unless there is some strong interest present, which in the meantime we are assuming to be absent, more than the mere attraction of attention by these means is necessary. The attention must be attracted in the direction of what is the real object of the advertisement; otherwise the advertisement may entirely fail to produce the effect it is intended to produce practically. For example, striking colours or contrast effects may be used in such a way as to attract attention to themselves, rather than to the article advertised; lettering may be used in 'hoarding' advertisements which is so large, that, while each individual letter attracts attention, the words themselves are never read, unless by the more or less accidental arousal of curiosity. In such cases the real aim of the advertisements is defeated.

These two ways of attracting attention really give us two different types of advertisement. Both can usually be found in the advertisement columns of any newspaper or periodical; but the one is characteristically the advertisement of the newspaper, the other of the railway station or hoarding. The one assumes a certain direction of interest so strong as to lead an individual to read an advertisement, if his attention is once attracted to the subject. The other assumes no such interest, and appeals for attention to its main points by the vividness, or other similar quality, of the impression; it may of course attempt to create an interest, but we are not concerned with that point just now. X appeals to, and can reach, A and B by the first form of advertisement; he must generally rely on the second form to reach C and D.

Newspapers and periodicals, in charging for advertisements, usually base the charge on the space occupied. Their point of view is easily understood. But it is interesting to consider whether the value to the advertiser of a full-page advertisement is really double the value of a half-page advertisement. Other things being equal, the appeal of the impression in each case depends on the size of the stimulus. But in what proportion? In the meantime we are considering the matter simply from the point of view of the appeal to attention, and assessing the value accordingly. Some experiments by W. D. Scott in America[1] with the object of testing

[1] See *The Psychology of Advertising*, p. 166.

this very point brought out rather striking results. He constructed a book of a hundred pages from advertisements cut from various magazines. These advertisements referred to a variety of different articles, but they were as nearly as possible equal in their appeal, except for size. The advertisements were full-page, half-page, quarter-page, and eight-page. Fifty individuals, who were ignorant of the aim of the experiment, were asked to glance over the pages of the book in the same way as they would look through the advertising pages of a magazine. They were instructed to take about ten minutes for the process, and at the end to write down what they had seen advertised.

Expressing the number of times the quarter-page advertisements were mentioned by unity, the results gave a value of six and a half for the full-page, less than three for the half-page, and about one-seventh for the one-eighth-page. That is to say, the full-page advertiser, though he pays twice as much as the half-page advertiser, makes the better bargain since he gets more than twice the value, and a still better bargain as compared with any of the others. For he pays four times as much as the quarter-page advertiser, and gets more than six times the value, and though he pays only eight times as much as the one-eighth-page advertiser, he gets more than forty times the value. All this, of course, is valid only on the assumption that we are concerned solely with the chance of attracting notice of a single advertisement, making no appeal except one dependent on size.

The attracting of the attention is obviously not the only result which an advertisement is intended to produce. The advertiser aims also at impressing something on the memory. It is clear that in a great number of cases—cases of people like C and D more especially—the advertiser must act on the assumption that the prospective buyer is hardly like to go straight away and purchase the article, when he has seen the advertisement, but that he will buy at some subsequent time if he buys at all. Hence the need of impressing the memory. One of the objects of attracting the attention, indeed, is in order to impress the memory.

The conditions already mentioned in connexion with attracting the attention are conditions which also hold with respect to impressing the memory. Hence the results of the experimental investigation we have just described might also be cited as illustrating the effect of the size of advertisements on the memory. But there are two important additional conditions, which must be mentioned here, and which from this point of view may exercise a much greater influence than mere size. In the first place, the subject of the advertisement must lend itself to easy remembering. An unfamiliar foreign word, for example, which has no associations in the mind, when used for the name of an article advertised, might attract the attention at the time, but would have comparatively little chance of being remembered. Or, again, the structure and form of the advertisement may be such that the characteristic content—that is, the name of the article and the producer—is forgotten, though the advertisement may be remembered as a vague whole.

In the second place, impression upon the memory depends to a very considerable extent upon repetition. A very interesting continuation of the advertising experiment we have described was made at Harvard, with the object of comparing the effect of repetition with the effect of relative size. Advertisements of full-page, half-page, quarter-page, and one-eighth-page size were taken as before, but they were arranged in such a way as to give equal total space to each advertisement. That is to say, for every once a full-page advertisement was given, a half-page was given twice, a quarter-page four times, and a one-eighth-page eight times. Care was taken that the same advertisement should never be repeated on the same page. The results of this experiment showed that the four-times-repeated quarter-page advertisement had fifty per cent more 'memory value' as compared with the once repeated full-page advertisement. But, as the size of the advertisement was further decreased, the 'memory value' did not rise above this figure. That is to say, there was a definite limit to the 'memory value' that could be obtained by decreasing the size and proportionately increasing the number of repetitions, and the maximum value was obtained for a quarter-size with four times the number of repetitions. A modification of the experiment gave still more striking results. In the whole experiment the subjects were asked to write down the names and articles they remembered. Some came readily, some only after considerable effort to recall. The modification consisted in reckoning only the first ten on each subject's list, thus taking the readiness with which an advertisement was recalled as an indication of the likelihood of its being recalled without special effort, and as measuring its effective 'memory value'. On calculating the results on this basis for the thirty subjects concerned, the investigators found that the 'memory value' of the four-times-repeated quarter-page advertisement was more than five times that of the once-repeated full-page advertisement, but, again, this represented the maximum value. The factors upon which the effectiveness of an advertisement depends are therefore somewhat complex. But, if we can take the results of these investigations as valid and reliable, and if the impressing of the memory so as to be readily recalled afterwards is the chief point to be considered in an advertisement, the practical deduction may be drawn that the merchant or manufacturer, who inserts one full-page advertisement in a paper does not get nearly so good a return for his expenditure as the merchant who inserts a quarter-page advertisement four times in different issues of the same paper—that is, on the assumption that charges are proportional to space, and that the regular circulation of the paper is of greater significance than the chance occasional circulation.

These investigations have been cited at length not merely for the results obtained, but also to show how readily the problems of advertising lend themselves to experimental treatment under laboratory conditions. It would be quite as easy to study the effect of other characteristics and features, as for example, the kind of lettering, the ease or difficulty of apprehension, colour schemes, contrast effects, and so on. As a matter of fact a very considerable amount of this kind of work has been done in America.

A third effect which an advertisement produces or is intended to produce is, perhaps, the most important effect of all. That is the stimulation of the will to buy, which we might apparently regard as the chief end of the advertisement. This cannot, however, be regarded as the sole end. It must not be forgotten that the will to buy depends in many cases upon factors with which advertising may have nothing whatever to do. In the case of people like A and B it is already developed, and all the advertiser aims at is to give it special direction. Only in the case of people like D is it entirely undeveloped. Hence, in considering this third effect, we must keep this group of prospective buyers specially in mind.

There are two main ways in which an advertisement can stimulate the will to buy. It can do so, on the one hand, by appeal to some relatively strong tendency—either characteristic of human nature itself, like some of our instinctive tendencies, or characteristic of a special class, group, or type of individual—such as, shall we say, vanity, superstition, the desire to get a bargain and the like. It can stimulate the will to buy, on the other hand, through the operation of suggestion, which may either reinforce an appeal directed to an existing tendency of the kind indicated, or may, to a certain extent, act on its own account and independently. To discuss the first way might be interesting, but would involve us in a somewhat lengthy consideration of a rather complex mass of details, and would yield us little in the way of general principles. It is better, therefore, in the present instance to confine our attention to the second.

We must first get a clear idea of the psychological phenomena of suggestion, and the factors upon which its operation and efficacy depend. Without going into needless technicalities, we may define suggestion as a process by which an individual's beliefs, ideas, or opinions, may be directed, modified, and controlled, independently of logical or rational grounds, and in such a way that the individual will act on such beliefs and opinions with at least as much certainty as he would act on beliefs and opinions for which he had logical grounds. The fact is, that it is only by reflection that we can distinguish in ourselves between beliefs and opinions to which we have come as a result of suggestion, and beliefs and opinions for which we have rational grounds. The phenomena of suggestion all depend on the fact that the suggested idea does not call up by association opposing ideas, is accepted therefore as a belief, and is acted upon. The extent to which opposing ideas can be kept from rising in the mind is always a measure of the force of a suggestion. The whole process may be described as a process of conveying ideas to another, and at the same time preventing opposing ideas arising, with a view to establishing beliefs and influencing action.

The phenomena of suggestion are best exhibited in the condition we call the hypnotic state, which may be regarded and described as a state of exaggerated suggestibility, brought about by particular circumstances. These means do not concern us at present. The phenomena themselves are not confined to the hypnotic state, but are widely prevalent in ordinary everyday life under normal conditions. Usually suggestion is an element in personal influence, that is, in the influence one person exerts on another because of certain personal characteristics. Again, the phenomena of personal suggestion are not those with which we are in the meantime concerned. The personal element even is by no means essential. Suggestive ideas can be conveyed in other ways than through personal intercourse. Suggestive value may be said to attach to anything which gives ideas, as it were, the run of consciousness, which prevents the rising into consciousness of opposing ideas, no matter whether this has a personal source or not.

Further suggestion may be either direct or indirect, and both kinds may be employed in advertisements. In indirect suggestion, the suggestion itself is as far as possible kept in the background. The aim is to create a mental background which will itself give rise to the idea or belief intended, but in such a way that the individual, who is the object of the suggestion, thinks the idea or belief is his own, and remains quite unconscious of the suggestion as such. This is the more difficult form of suggestion to employ, but when skil-fully employed is likely to be the more successful, especially with those people—and they are fairly numerous—who tend to resent any attempt to influence their actions by suggestion, and to take exactly the opposite view or course of action from that suggested. Direct suggestion explains itself. This is the conveying of the idea or opinion to another without any attempt at disguise, and is the easier and the more usual method of operation.

As far as advertising, as distinguished from personal influence, is concerned, both kinds of suggestion, but especi-ally the second, depend upon two sets of conditions—conditions affecting the source or origin of the suggestion, including in this case the manner in which it is conveyed, and conditions affecting the individual to whom the suggestion comes. Anything which gives impressiveness or vividness or weight to the original idea will tend to give it suggestive value. Thus the conditions upon which the attracting of attention depend are also conditions which favour suggestion. The mere repetition of a name or statement tends to give suggestive value. Repetition may give suggestive value in two different ways. The more frequently a statement is made, the greater is our tendency to accept and believe it. On this principle the German news agencies persistently acted throughout the two World Wars. On the other hand, an article, the name or maker's name of which is familiar to us, will in general be preferred to a similar article which may even be better suited to our purpose, but the name of which is unfamiliar. To include this case is possibly to use sug-gestion in a rather wide sense. The mere recognition of a familiar name seems to be pleasant. We feel, as it were, in the presence of an old friend. Whether this has suggestive value or not in the strict sense, it undoubtedly operates in pretty much the same way.

Further, the form in which a statement is made has a suggestive value of its own. The simple imperative, 'Use Brook's Soap,' may possibly lose some of its virtue in the long run if it is too frequently employed. But there is a

great variety of similar statements available, by all of which
a suggestion may be conveyed and by some with more
efficacy than the simple imperative can claim. 'Are you using
Brook's Soap?' 'Are you not using Brook's Soap?' 'Brook's
Soap is the best', 'Is not Brook's Soap the best?' and similar
variants, might be cited in illustration. Even the individual
who resents direct suggestion and takes the opposite course
might be ensnared by a skilful use of negatives.

The conditions favourable to suggestion, which affect the
individual to whom the suggestion comes, are also numerous.
In the first place there are individual differences in liability
to be influenced by suggestion in general. In the second
place there are individual characteristics, tendencies, desires,
to which appeal may be made by certain forms of advertisement or certain advertised articles; and, since we frequently
believe what we wish to believe, such appeal will aid the
suggestion conveyed. In the third place there are attitudes of
mind, states of health, and so on, which will afford a suitable
background for the development of certain suggestions.

All the three effects of advertisements which we have noted
must be considered by X, the would-be seller. He will lay
stress on those characteristics which produce mainly the
effect suitable to the case of the buyer or buyers upon whom
he relies. Thus if he desires to appeal to buyers of the type
of A, all that he requires to do is to advertise the fact that he
sells a certain article of a certain quality. Hence he will
concentrate attention on the first effect. For the appeal to
buyers of the type of B, the main emphasis must also be on
the first effect, but there is also some need for the third effect.
For the appeal to buyers of the type of C, emphasis must be
laid mainly on the third effect, while for buyers of the type
of D, the third is again of chief importance, but the second
is also important.

Before leaving the subject of advertising, there is one other
point which is worthy of receiving some attention on our
part. To some extent it has been already more or less tacitly
assumed. There seems to be a practically universal demand
on the part of the buying public for some concrete symbol or

specific name by which to mark and recognize the objects which express or satisfy needs and desires. The demand appears to arise from a general tendency of human nature. At all events there is no doubting its reality. The manufacturer or merchant, though he has probably never reflected on the psychological meaning and significance of the demand, is quite awake to the concrete reality in practice. Accordingly he has his 'trade mark', and in most cases he goes beyond this, and 'christens' the article he puts on the market by some specific name. The choice of a suitable name is itself an important problem, on which the psychology of advertising may have something helpful to contribute, and the methods of the psychological laboratory may readily be pressed into service. Most of what we have said about advertising in general will in fact be found to apply. In other words this is simply a special aspect of advertising.

There is an aspect, however, of the 'trade mark' or 'trade name', which has been the subject of experimental investigation in the psychological laboratory, to which we have not yet referred. Cases of alleged infringement of the rights in a registered 'trade mark' or name are not infrequent in our law-courts. It is exceedingly difficult to determine the principles upon which decision in such a matter can or ought to be based, and this difficulty is reflected in the apparent want of consistency shown by decisions actually given. Thus in cases in America 'Non-X-Ell' was decided to be an infringement of 'Nox-all', 'Autola' of 'Au-to-do', 'Green Ribbon' of 'Green River', whereas 'Kalodont' was decided not to be an infringement of 'Sozodont', 'Veribest' not to be an infringement of 'Bestyette', 'Pinozyme' not to be an infringement of 'Peptenzyme'. Paynter arranged an experiment in which he asked the subjects to say whether each of a series of 'trade names' presented one at a time was identical or not with a name seen on a previous occasion. In some cases the names were identical, in others imitated more or less closely. The degree of confusion between two or more less similar names was measured by the number of times they were taken for one another under these conditions. In several cases pairs of names were included, when a legal decision on the question of infringement was extant, as with those given above. The results are interesting from the point of view of a comparison between the legal decision, and the amount of confusion as determined in this way. In the 'Nox-all' case the percentage of confusion was 28, in the 'Sozodont' case it was exactly the same; in the 'Autola' case it was 40, and in 'Peptenzyme' it was 43. That is, in two cases where the risk of confusion appears, on the results of the experiment, to be exactly equal, opposite decisions were given; and in the other two cases, that where the risk of confusion was shown to be the less was decided to be an infringement, and that where the risk was the greater to be not an infringement. The moral would appear to be that in these commercially important legal cases, the decisions given are largely arbitrary, and possibly determined by chance circumstances, when a reliable psychological test could without difficulty be applied.[1]

Advertising is not the only method which our would-be seller X can employ, and does employ, in order to secure buyers for the articles he wishes to sell. We have yet to consider from the psychological point of view another method of bringing about the reaction we call buying and selling, the method typified by the shop-window display, and also exemplified in the illustrated catalogue, the sample packet, and so on. In order to prevent confusion we may confine our attention to the window display, but the principles apply to all varieties of this type or group of methods.

The effects which the window display is intended to produce are effects with which we are already familiar, but in this case the appeal to the memory is of relatively minor significance. The two main effects to be produced are the attracting of the attention, and the stimulation of the will to buy. The general characteristics or features in a window display, which will secure these two effects, are not very different from those already discussed or mentioned as the

[1] Quoted from Hollingworth and Poffenberger, *Applied Psychology*, p. 237.

features of advertisements. Lighting, colour, and arrangement are the main points to be considered in connexion with the attempt to attract attention to the window display as a whole. Arrangement is the chief consideration as regards attracting attention to individual articles, and with reference to the stimulation of the will to buy.

Moreover, a window display, in order to attract attention and stimulate the will to buy, must possess the characteristic we might describe by the term 'interesting'. What is interesting to one individual, or group or class of individuals, may not be in the least degree interesting, may even be repulsive, to another individual, group, or class. Hence we find that a window display is generally characteristic of the public for whom a particular merchant caters. Nevertheless the quality 'interestingness' must always depend mainly on the articles displayed and their arrangement. It is very important to remember that, to make a shop window 'interesting', it is not necessary to make it artistically or aesthetically beautiful. We cannot determine the practical value of a window display by aesthetic standards. In fact a psychologist would say that the more nearly perfect a display is from the purely aesthetic point of view, the less likely it is to stimulate buying, however much it may attract attention. This may be contrary to general opinion, and even to some of the statements of trade books on the subject. But it certainly seems to the psychologist to be a true statement nevertheless.

The point is worth emphasizing. The more perfect a display is from the aesthetic point of view, the more are we likely to be satisfied with simply looking at it, and the less likely are we to have practical designs with respect to any of the exhibited articles. Of course there may be exceptions, but this would seem to be the general rule. On the other hand the ugly and repulsive will undoubtedly repel us, and the feeling of displeasure may attach to the objects. Hence the window display, in order to avoid this danger, must at least be tasteful and pleasant. Moreover, attention should be directed and focused on the goods exhibited, and these should be made to appear individually as attractive as possible. This mere fact involves the denial of the possibility of making the display an aesthetically perfect whole—in other words a work of art, in the strict meaning of art. The practical art of window-dressing consists first of all in securing that the attention and interest of the passer-by should be attracted by a striking, pleasant, and tasteful, but not necessarily artistically beautiful, display, and then, in the second place in evoking in the passer-by the desire to become the possessor of some one of the articles displayed by the suggestiveness of the arrangement, and the way in which the attractiveness of the article in question is enhanced.

The same principles hold of the packings, covers, wrappings, and labels, with which goods are sent into the market. Münsterberg[1] cites a curious case which seems to prove that artistic beauty of label has little to do with the sale of an article. A firm of confectioners sold a certain kind of chocolate in twelve different packets, and under twelve different labels. In all cases the labels were decorated with the same kind of pictures—pictures of women with scenic backgrounds. Artistically the labels were all on practically the same footing and level. Yet one of the labels was highly successful over the whole country, a second had made precisely the same article almost unsaleable, while the other ten could be graded between these two extremes according to their sale value. Here surely is a fruitful field for psychological work. Some has been done, but there is much still to do.

In certain cases the suggestive value of a window display may be considerably heightened by the mere appearance of quantity or abundance which it represents. The practical problem in this connexion will be very different for different tradesmen. In some cases it will not matter though the individual articles should be lost in the mass, as in the case of the fruit merchant displaying apples or oranges; and possibly these are the cases where the phenomenon is of greatest practical significance. On the other hand, there are

[1] *Op. cit.*, p. 279.

cases, such as that of the jeweller, where the impression of abundance must be given, but at the same time the individual articles must not be allowed to lose themselves in the mass, but must attract attention individually. A theoretical psychology cannot of course solve the problem of either the fruiterer or the jeweller, but the problem is nevertheless largely a psychological problem, that ought in practice to be approached from the psychological point of view. That the psychologist could devise experiments, the results of which would go far in the direction of furnishing the required solution in any particular case, is certain.

But what of our four prospective buyers and this new kind of attempt on the part of X to induce them to buy his articles? The situation is very much the same as in the case of advertisements. For individuals of the A type the attracting of attention is the main thing; for those of the D type the suggestive effect is the prime consideration. For the others both effects are important, but with slightly different emphasis. The emphasis is on the first effect with individuals like B, on the second effect with individuals of the type of C.

CHAPTER XII

THE ART OF THE SALESMAN

IN the last chapter we considered the various ways in which a would-be seller, X, might seek to influence different types of prospective buyers, by means of advertising, display, and the like, with a view to bringing about the buying-selling reaction. Four types of buyers were distinguished—the buyer A with the will to buy and with complete and definite knowledge of what he wants, the buyer B also with the will to buy, but only a general idea of the kind of thing he wants, the buyer C with money which he desires to spend but only the vaguest notion even of the kind of thing on which he ought to spend it, and the buyer D who is merely not unwilling to buy. We have still to consider the art of the salesman itself. It is clear that the art of the salesman need only concern itself with prospective buyers of the types B and C. The buyer of the type A is already so far advanced towards buying that there is little room for the salesman's art, while the buyer of the type D, so long as he remains at the standpoint of D, will seldom give the salesman any opportunity of displaying his skill.

The psychological conditions which favour the art of the salesman are once more the conditions we have already considered in the last chapter with reference to advertising and display, and the two main effects which the art produces are, as before, the attraction of the attention of the prospective buyer and the stimulation of the will to buy. It is evident that the salesman, if he has an active function to perform at all, must on the one hand direct his activity towards attracting the attention of the prospective buyer to an article or to certain articles, and then, through suggestion or otherwise, as opportunity offers, towards guiding the thinking and resolving of the buyer in such a way as to stimulate the will to buy. If a salesman does not do these things, then an automatic delivery machine would do his work much better and more economically, and would also obviate the danger of distracting the attention of a buyer away from an article at the very moment when he is about to buy it.

There are two characteristic and essential features in the psychological situation when the art of the salesman comes upon the scene. In the first place there is an introduction of the personal element. This opens up the possibility of bringing personal influence to bear, and this in turn opens a new avenue for the operation of suggestion, and affords an additional opportunity of influencing the buyer by way of the process psychologists call *sympathy*.

As far as suggestion is concerned there is not a great deal to be added to what has already been said. In this case, however, the source of the suggestion is a person. Personal prestige will now give added weight to suggested opinions or actions, and will in proportion enhance their suggestive value. Personal prestige may be due to all sorts of things. The general principle is that any superiority in another, provided it does not arouse antagonism or resentment, tends to put us in a receptive attitude towards him. Hence such prestige may be given by good appearance, fine dress, confident manner, superior knowledge, reputation, even superior size, and a number of other things, all of which might with advantage be considered by a merchant inter-viewing applicants for the position of salesman or sales-woman.

Sympathy we have not hitherto had occasion to mention, but it also is an important factor in personal influence. The psychologist does not use the word 'sympathy' in the ordinary popular sense, in which it is almost equivalent to 'pity', but in a sense more like the original meaning of 'feeling with'. When we see the signs of any feeling or emotion in other people, we have a tendency—which is practically universal —to experience the feelings and emotions ourselves of which we see the expressive signs, even though we should be entirely ignorant of the object which has evoked them in the other people. Thus, if an acquaintance, with whom we are conversing in the street, starts suddenly, or shows other symptoms of fear, we also experience a thrill of fear, even before we have looked round to see the cause. When we see a man stop when crossing a bridge or viaduct, and gaze down into a river or a road underneath, we always feel inclined to follow his example, and often we actually do so. This infectiousness of feeling or emotion, this tendency to communicate itself directly, the psychologist has long recognized, and he uses the word 'sympathy' to designate the tendency in the person who receives the feeling or emotion. It is evident that the actor and the orator rely very largely on this sympathy for their effects. The same is true, though in perhaps a minor degree, of the salesman. There are many cases where the interest and desire of a customer are aroused by a skilful display of the necessary enthusiasm on the part of the salesman, and a sale is in consequence effected which could not have been effected had there been a cold or lackadaisical attitude on his part. It must be remembered that it is not the words he employs, but the feeling attitudes he expresses in the way he speaks them, or in other ways, that can operate in this particular manner.

The second new and characteristic feature in the psychological situation is that the prospective buyer must be considered and treated as an individual, and the methods the salesman adapted to the circumstances of the particular case. A very great part of the ability of a salesman will depend on the extent to which he can—it may be unconsciously—take advantage of this peculiarity of the situation. Take the case of a prospective buyer of the C type entering a shop. He has only a general intention to buy, but no definite intention to buy a particular thing, or even a particular kind of thing. The issue is very open and the case apparently one in which almost any suggestion might determine the process of buying. On the other hand a chance suggestion might come up against a strong prejudice which C has, and be therefore in its effect worse than no suggestion at all; C might even have a strong prejudice against being influenced by suggestion at all, might resent very strongly any attempt to influence him by suggestion which he detected. Obviously under these circumstances a chance suggestion might have the effect of making C resist all subsequent attempts on the part of the salesman to induce him to buy anything.

From this point of view the first business of the salesman would appear to be to take his cue from the prospective buyer, to discover, if possible, in what direction his main interests lie, what, if any, characteristics or tendencies in him may be appealed to, how he reacts to suggestion, direct and indirect, and so on. The time spent in getting this knowledge—and with a skilful salesman and an ordinary customer it is usually very short—is really time gained. For with such knowledge the salesman can almost infallibly direct a prospective buyer's attention in such a way that he becomes a real buyer, that is change type C first into B, then into A, and finally evoke the necessary reaction.

In this connexion it is perhaps worth while referring once more to the problem of vocational selection for salesmanship. It is clear that much of the success of the salesman must depend on certain particular qualities and traits, which are essentially natural rather than acquired. It is also clear that the devising of adequate tests for these qualities and traits would be a very valuable and economic service on the part of the psychologist. The work is being assiduously pursued at the present time in several laboratories. We have already instanced the devising of a test of ability to remember and recognize faces. Such an ability would be very valuable from precisely that point of view which we have just considered. In the same way tests of other and equally valuable traits and abilities might be devised.

There are a few other points deserving of notice, some of which we often find neglected in our ordinary shopping experience. Nothing wastes more time in a shop than the dissipating of the attention of a prospective buyer when it has once been gained by a particular article, and when the buying is on the point of taking place. This is very frequently done by exhibiting and bringing to the notice of the customer a number of other articles, and so causing the whole effect of the work up to that time to be lost. Some salesmen indeed exhibit articles in such a way as to prevent the attention ever becoming fixed. This is probably done of set purpose, in some instances, as a method of practically forcing inferior goods on an unwary buyer. Even where it is not done of set purpose it may have the result of sending a buyer away with something that does not meet his needs nearly so well as something else he had been previously shown. In either case the policy is obviously shortsighted. For the best and surest effect from the salesman's point of view, and for the most satisfactory outcome from the buyer's, the exhibition of articles should be carefully designed and calculated, not merely indiscriminate. Further, the gestures of the salesman may have the effect of distracting attention from goods, as well as calling attention to them, and the tone in which he speaks of any articles may exercise as much influence as the words spoken.

In the work of the salesman there is practically nothing so unimportant as to be entirely negligible. This principle always holds where personal influence is a determining factor. In a large American establishment employing some hundreds of saleswomen it was thought that the expense for the delivery of articles sold formed far too large an item in the expenditure. The saleswomen had been in the habit of asking every purchaser, even when the articles were small, the question: 'May we send it for you?' They were instructed to substitute for this in the case of small articles the question: 'Will you take it with you?' This apparently insignificant change, a change in suggestion, which probably not one person in a thousand ever noticed, made a very considerable difference in the expenditure of the business in the course of the year.

It may sound absurd in the ears of a Britisher to say that salesmen should be trained systematically, and that psychology should form an important part of the training, both general psychology and the special psychology of salesmanship. But the Americans do not find it absurd. Before many years have elapsed there will be as little absurdity in the suggestion on this as on the other side of the Atlantic.

Although in this and the previous chapter we have been considering the process of buying and selling from the point of view of the interest and effort of the seller, the discussion had also had its lessons for the buyer. In concluding this chapter we might profitably gather those lessons together, and point the moral. In order to buy satisfactorily, the buyer must buy what he needs and wants, and he must buy at a price which is not excessive, reckoning in the price not merely the money paid but the time and trouble expended as well. It ought to be noted that as a rule it is the interest of the regular seller to suit both the buyer's needs and his purse. It is only the incidental seller, or the shopkeeper who depends mainly on a passing trade, that can afford to neglect the interest of the buyer. In such cases, therefore, the danger of buying the wrong thing and the danger of buying at an excessive price are at their maximum. But in every case the danger is present to some extent, for after all the seller must be presumed to seek primarily his own interest. The extent of the danger will depend very considerably on the individuality of the buyer. If the buyer is highly suggestible, if he has certain strong tendencies to which an appeal can easily be made—bargain-hunting for example—the first essential in his own interest is that he should be conscious of these weaknesses, and therefore on his guard against the results to which they may lead. The extent of the danger depends also on the particular determination of the will in the case of the buyer. A buyer of type A is in a relatively safe position. He has a definite want, and knows definitely what will satisfy that want. With buyers of the other three types, B, C, and D, the danger becomes progressively greater as their knowledge of what will suit them becomes less and less definite, and their intentions also of course less clearly defined, since both these conditions favour the process of suggestion as we have seen.

Lack of knowledge with regard to any subject also renders

an individual suggestible with respect to that subject, when in the presence of some one who seems to know all about it. That is a general psychological principle. Hence definite knowledge of the article we buy is another important safeguard against the unscrupulous seller. It is all mainly a matter of knowledge, together with some training and practice in the use of our knowledge. Knowledge of our own weaknesses, knowledge of what we really want, knowledge of the article in question, and some knowledge of the psychological processes involved in buying, selling, advertising, and display, even though it be merely empirical knowledge in every case, are the chief safeguards against buying what we do not want or require, buying a worthless article, and buying at too high a price—these together with some slight knowledge of the seller.

There may some day be an applied psychology of the consumer from the consumer's point of view. In the meantime he must be content with the existing applied psychology of salesmanship from the seller's point of view. As we pointed out at the start, buying and selling are the names we give to two aspects of the one process, and most topics treated in the psychology of salesmanship have also the two aspects. In fact the psychology of salesmanship and advertising is very largely the psychology of the consumer, except for that section which deals with vocational testing for salesmanship, and even here the consumer must necessarily come into the picture.

The psychology of salesmanship is in fact very largely a direct application of the principles of general psychology, not a highly specialized branch like industrial psychology. Recently the author had occasion to make the necessary arrangements to enable an American research student to continue the work he had been doing at Columbia University. He was working on the psychology of salesmanship, and the piece of work he actually did in Edinburgh consisted in an investigation of the superstitions of some two hundred students. The relation to salesmanship at first seems farfetched, but only until we realize it. This work was a logical continuation of the work he had already done. It illustrates with sufficient clearness and emphasis the extent to which the psychology of salesmanship is the psychology of the consumer, that is, of the ordinary, everyday human being.

CHAPTER XIII

CONCLUSION

IT ought to be clearly understood that the applications of psychology with which we have been dealing do not by any means stand alone. The psychology of industry and commerce is only one aspect or direction of a wider movement, as we have already tried to show. And this movement is a rapidly developing one. There is a great deal of talk just now about a 'new' psychology. The reference is usually to Freudian psychology. But the real new psychology is much wider than the Freudian and kindred developments. Some of these developments may be 'new', but they are certainly not psychology. Where they are entitled to be recognized by that science, they are to be placed side by side with other developments no less significant, and all characteristic of the real new psychology, among which must be included the applied psychology of industry and the applied psychology of education.

What is really characteristic of the new psychology is a changed attitude towards the facts and phenomena studied. So important is this point, that, at the risk of repetition, we must once more draw attention to it. What psychology seeks to study and understand is human nature in the widest sense, as manifesting itself in human behaviour. There are two possible standpoints from which we may seek to understand human nature. On the one hand we may desire to gain some light on the nature and destiny of the human soul, and we study human behaviour and mental process with that as our main end. The attitude is a perfectly legitimate one, and the end a very reasonable and proper end. Such was the attitude and end of the old psychology. On the other hand we may study human nature and mental process in order to gain an insight into human behaviour, and in order practically to control human behaviour and make it more efficient, in our own case as well as in the case of other people. This is the attitude and end of the new psychology. It is also a perfectly legitimate attitude and a reasonable end.

The change has, however, been a tremendously significant one for psychology itself as a science. The scope of the science has widened enormously, and with the widened scope new methods of study have been developed and elaborated. The science has also taken its place alongside of its kindred sciences. And finally the practical applicability of its findings have become immediately obvious. Time was when men regarded a too close scrutiny of nature as savouring of impiety. There may be some now who regard the closer scrutiny of mental process in the same light, or even perhaps as sacrilege. But the new way of looking at the world of material phenomena has amply justified itself, as will the new way of regarding mental phenomena in the not very distant future.

When, in 1913, Münsterberg published his *Psychology and Industrial Efficiency*, he was a pioneer in a new field, but he realized that psychology must soon come to its own in that field, though it is doubtful if he realized how soon. It has already come to its own in America; it is coming to its own on this side of the Atlantic. At the end of the First World War the National Institute of Industrial Psychology, already referred to, was established, with the object of organizing the efforts to apply psychology to industry and commerce, and to develop the work systematically. As we have indicated considerable developments have taken place since then. In industry and commerce, therefore, no less than in education and in medicine, the value of the new psychology for the practical needs of a practical world is coming to be recognized.

Hence we may without hesitation claim that the new psychology has already made good in the two ways in which it is demanded that a science should make good—in the extending of human knowledge of the phenomena studied and of the laws in accordance with which the phenomena occur in orderly sequence and mutual interdependence, on the one hand, and in the practical value of that knowledge for human life and activity, on the other. If the omens are to be relied on the future will see a psychology of still wider scope and of still greater service to humanity.

One last word. The issues facing this country in the fifth decade of the twentieth century are gradually defining themselves. He would be blind indeed, who failed to see the chasm that has opened between the Britain of to-day and the Britain of 1900, as a result of the two World Wars. Whatever other effects may show themselves, it is certain that socially and economically the changes will be profound. A great creditor nation has become a debtor nation. A great importing nation—and necessarily so—must now make a complete reversal, as regards the ratio of its imports to its exports. Everything stresses the fact that from now on our dependence must be upon ourselves, on the health, mental ability, knowledge and skill of the inhabitants of this island. The conservation and full utilization of that part of our national wealth is clearly imperative. Need more be said for the importance of a psychology of industry?

APPENDIX I

SOME USEFUL BOOKS BEARING UPON THE PSYCHOLOGY OF INDUSTRY AND COMMERCE

ADAMS, H. F. *Advertising and its Natural Laws*, Macmillan, New York, 1916.

ARAI, T. *Mental Fatigue.* Columbia Univ. Press, New York, 1912.

ASH, I. E. *Fatigue and its Effect upon Control.* Archives of Psychology, No. 31. 1914.

BARTLETT, F. C. *The Psychology of the Soldier.* Camb. Univ. Press, 1927.

BINET and SIMON. *The Development of Intelligence in Children.* Vineland, 1916.

BRETT, H. E. *Psychology and Industrial Efficiency.* New York, 1920.

BRISCO, NORRIS A. *Fundamentals of Salesmanship.* Appleton, New York, 1916.

CHAPMAN, J. C. *Trade Tests.* Holt, New York, 1921.

DAWSON, S. *An Introduction to the Computation of Statistics.* Lond. Univ. Press, 1933.

DRURY, H. B. *Scientific Management.* Columbia Univ. Press, New York, 1918.

FLORENCE, P. S. *Economics of Fatigue and Unrest.* Holt, New York, 1924.

FREDERICK, CHRISTINE. *The New Housekeeping.* Doubleday, Page, New York, 1913.

GILBRETH, F. B. and L. M. *Fatigue Study.* London, 1917.

GILBRETH, F. B. and L. M. *Applied Motion Study.* New York.

GILBRETH, L. M. *The Psychology of Management.* Stringer and Walton, New York, 1918.

HOLLINGWORTH, H. L. *Advertising and Selling.* Appleton, New York, 1912.

HOLLINGWORTH, H. L. *Vocational Psychology and Character Analysis.* Appleton, New York, 1929.

HULL, C. L. *Aptitude Testing.* New York, 1928.

Industrial Health (formerly Industrial Fatigue) Research Board Reports. H.M. Stationery Office, London. V.D.

KENAGY, H. S., and YOAKUM, C. S. *Selection and Training of Salesmen.* New York, 1925.

KORNHAUSER, C. W., and KINGSBURY, G. A. *Psychological Tests in Business.* Chicago Univ. Press, 1924.

LEE, F. S. *The Human Machine and Industrial Efficiency.* Longmans, New York, 1918.

LEVERHULME, LORD. *The Six-hour Day.* Allen & Unwin, London, 1918.

LINK, H. C. *Employment Psychology.* Macmillan Co., New York, 1919.

MCCLELLAND, W. W. *Selection for Secondary Education.* London Univ. Press, 1942.

MCDOUGALL, W. *Introduction to Social Psychology.* 22nd ed., Methuen, London, 1931.

MCKILLOP, M. and A. D. *Efficiency Methods.* London, 1917.

MACMEEKEN, A. M. *The Intelligence of a Representative Group of Scottish Children.* London Univ. Press, 1939.

MELVILLE, N. J. *Testing Juvenile Mentality.* Philadelphia, 1917.

MÜNSTERBERG, H. *Psychology and Industrial Efficiency.* Constable, London, 1913.

MUSCIO, B. *Lectures on Industrial Psychology.* Routledge, London, 1920.

MYERS, C. S. *Mind and Work.* London Univ. Press, 1920.

MYERS, C. S. *Industrial Psychology in Great Britain.* London, 1920.

MYERS, C. S. (Editor). *Industrial Psychology.* Home Univ. Press, 1929.

PATRICK, G. T. W. *The Psychology of Relaxation.* Houghton Mifflin Co., Boston, 1916.

PEAR, T. H. *Skill in Work and Play.* London, 1924.

POFFENBERGER, A. T. *Applied Psychology.* Appleton, New York, 1927.

SCOTT, W. D. *Psychology of Advertising.* Small, Maynard & Co., Boston, 1908.

SCOTT, W. D. *Theory of Advertising.* Small, Maynard & Co., Boston, 1913.

Scottish Council for Research in Education. Report No. V. *The Intelligence of Scottish Children.* London Univ. Press, 1934.

STARCH, D. *Advertising.* Scott, Foreman & Co., Chicago, 1914.

STRONG, E. K. *Relative Merits of Advertisements.* Science Press, New York, 1911.

SWIFT, E. J. *Psychology of the Day's Work.* Appleton, New York, 1919.

SYMONDS, N. M. *Diagnosing Personality and Conduct.* New York, 1932.

TAYLOR, F. W. *Principles of Scientific Management.* Harper's, New York, 1915.

TEAD, ORDWAY. *Instinct in Industry.* Houghton Mifflin Co. (Constable), Boston, 1918.

TERMAN, L. M. *The Measurement of Intelligence.* Harrap, London, 1919.

VERNON, H. M. *Industrial Fatigue and Efficiency.* London, 1921.

VITELES, M. S. *Industrial Psychology.* Cape, London, 1932.

WATTS, FRANK. *An Introduction to the Psychological Problems of Industry.* Allen & Unwin, London, 1921.

WHIPPLE, G. M. *Manual of Mental and Physical Tests.* Warwick and York (Harrap), Baltimore, 1914.

WHITEHEAD, H. *Principles of Salesmanship.* Ronald Press, New York, 1917.

YERKES, BRIDGES, and HARDWICK. *A Point Scale for Measuring Mental Ability.* Warwick & York, Baltimore, 1915.

YOAKUM and YERKES. *Mental Tests in the American Army.* London, 1920.

APPENDIX II

A FOOT-RULE FOR INTELLIGENCE TESTING

THE tests here given are not intended to serve in any way as a standard scale, but merely as an abbreviated scale for preliminary work. The Binet scale itself may be regarded as of the nature of a first aid, rather than a scale for accurate measurement. But it is too long and cumbrous for use as a first aid unless for cases fairly low down the scale. The tests here given are meant, then, to serve as such a first aid for all levels.

In using the tests the experimenter should start from the beginning and go on until the subject fails in all the tests except the second and third. In these cases the indication of mental age is given at once. In order to obtain the approximate mental age of the subject, take the mean level attained in the six tests.

TEST 1. MEMORY SPAN FOR DIGITS

Begin with	3 digits	Corresponding mental age			3
	4 ,,	,,	,,	,,	4
	3 backwards	,,	,,	,,	7
	4 ,,	,,	,,	,,	9
	6 forwards	,,	,,	,,	10
	5 backwards	,,	,,	,,	12
	7 forwards	,,	,,	,,	14
	6 backwards	,,	,,	,,	adult

TEST 2. VOCABULARY

The simplest way to test vocabulary is by using Terman's list of words. The number of words known indicates mental age.

20 words indicates age			8
30 ,,	,,	,,	10
40 ,,	,,	,,	12
50 ,,	,,	,,	14
65 ,,	,,	,,	adult

TEST 3. PICTURE TEST

Simple enumeration of objects indicates mental age 3
Description   ,,   ,,   ,,   7
Interpretation   ,,   ,,   ,,   12

TEST 4. COMPREHENSION OF SITUATION

Comprehension is tested by an intelligent answer to the question asked.

What ought you to do when you are sleepy?
What ought you to do when you are cold?
What ought you to do when you are hungry?   Age 4
What ought you to do if it is raining when you start for school?
What ought you to do if you find that your house is on fire?
What ought you to do if you are going somewhere and miss your train?   Age 6
What ought you to do when you have broken something belonging to another?
What ought you to do when you notice on your way to school that you are in danger of being late?
What ought you to do if a playmate hits you without meaning it?   Age 8
What ought you to say when someone asks your opinion about a person you do not know very well?
What ought you to do before beginning something very important?
Why should we judge a person more by what he does than by what he says?   Age 10
A man who was walking in the woods near a city stopped suddenly, very much frightened, and then ran to the nearest policeman and said that he had just seen hanging from the branch of a tree a . . . what?
My neighbour has been having strange visitors. First a doctor came to his house, then a lawyer, and then a minister. What do you think happened there?
An Indian, who had come to town for the first time, saw a white man riding along the street. As the white man rode past the Indian said, 'The white man is lazy; he walks sitting down.' What was the white man riding on?   Age 14

TEST 5. DEFINITIONS

Ability to name a key, a knife, a penny.	Age 3
Definition in terms of use of: fork, table, chair.	Age 5
Definitions superior to those in terms of use of same words.	Age 8
Definition of abstract words: revenge, charity, justice	Age 12
What are three differences between a president and a king?	Age 14

TEST 6. INGENUITY TEST

Ability to place together parts of rectangle divided into two along one diagonal.   **Age 5**

Ball and field puzzle (Terman) inferior solution.   **Age 8**

Ability to tell change that should be given back:

  On buying fourpence-worth of candy and giving the shopkeeper a shilling.

  On buying sixpence-worth and giving the shopkeeper a florin.   **Age 9**

Healy and Fernald's Form Board (Terman).   **Age 10**

Ball and field. Superior solution.   **Age 11**

Telling what time it would be if the hands of the clock were reversed if it is now 6.22.   **Age 14**

You see this box; it has two smaller boxes inside, and each of these contains a little box. How many boxes are there altogether?

A dairyman had an eight-pint measure full of milk. Two other measures were in the shop: a three-pint measure and a five-pint measure. He wished to divide the milk into two exactly equal portions of four pints each. How could he do that with the measures he had?   **Adult**

INDEX

For Product Safety Concerns and Information please contact our EU
representative GPSR@taylorandfrancis.com
Taylor & Francis Verlag GmbH, Kaufingerstraße 24, 80331 München, Germany